ly

Doreen Anne West

LOUIE: A Country Lady

This is the true story of Louie, a
country lady. It follows her married
life, sometimes tempestuous,
sometimes amusing, with a
background of two World Wars and
farming life as it was in rural
Oxfordshire.

Doreen Louie West

LOUIE
A COUNTRY LADY

The story of an Oxfordshire farming family

Nutty Books
68 Worminghall Road, Oakley, Bucks, HP18 9QY, U.K.
Tel: 01844 237417

First published in Great Britain 1997 by
Nutty Books
68 Worminghall Road, Oakley, Bucks, HP18 9QY, U.K.

Reprinted December, 1997
Reprinted January, 1998
Reprinted February, 1998

British Library Cataloguing-in-Publication Data.
A catalogue record for this book is available
from the British Library.

ISBN: 0-9531117-0-9

Printed by *Manuscript ReSearch Printing*
P.O. Box 33, Bicester, Oxon, OX6 7PP, England.
Telephone: 01869 323447   Fax: 01869 324096

ACKNOWLEDGEMENT

*My thanks go to everyone who has helped and encouraged me to write this book, particularly remembering **Pat Johnson,** who spent so many patient hours with her word processor.*

Doreen Louie West

ONE

On a winter's night in 1910 Louie was sitting by the embers of the fire as the last log crumbled and fell from the dog irons.

It was past midnight and the rain was beating against the window, she was waiting for her father to return from an evening out with a few farming friends. They would occasionally meet at the local inn, have a few drinks and a game of cards, but he had never been as late as this before and Louie was beginning to worry, not only about him, but the young lad, Jessy, who was waiting to attend to the horse. He had come to work at Draycot for Tom Latham on leaving school and loved the work, especially the horses.

Tom Latham, Louie's father, was a successful farmer and ran three farms, Goldpits Farm at Tetsworth, Harlesford at Stoke Talmage and Draycot near Shabbington. His first wife, Clementina, had died, leaving five children — Alice, Arthur, Lambourn, Dick and Louie.

Henrietta came to Draycot as governess to the children and had a mammoth task with five boisterous children all at different stages of education and desperately missing their mother. When, about two years after Clementina's death Tom married Henrietta, they tried not to show the resentment they felt, though Louie flatly refused to address her as mother, so it was agreed that they should all call her mater. Louie, by this time, had left school and was helping Henrietta to run the farmhouse,

Jessy would have to be at work by six o'clock next morning so they were both relieved to hear the sound of the horse and trap on the gravel drive.

While Louie was helping her father into the kitchen, Jessy took the horse round to the stable yard. "He is as tight as the proverbial tick." Louie had never seen her father quite so intoxicated before — sometimes a bit merry but never 'legless'. She helped him into a chair and pulled off his muddy boots, taking them into the scullery.

When she returned he was standing up and reaching for his double barrelled gun from the rack. She tried to bar his way as he stumbled towards the mantle shelf to the cartridge box, taking out two cartridges he loaded the gun and snapped it shut. "I think I will shoot you Louie," he said, pointing the gun in her direction. "I wouldn't if I were you, at least not until I have got you out of those wet clothes and it would wake mater".

Louie took the gun, broke it and removing the cartridges she put it back on the rack and turned to her father. "What a state you are in Dad." She pulled off his soaking overcoat.

He gave a rather sheepish grin, "I'll never make those bloody stairs but I will be up for milking in the morning".

"Never let your nights interfere with your mornings," said Louie, "you have told us that often enough".

Tom thought the world of Louie and she knew he would not have shot her but when the drink is in the sense is out and she resolved to hide the guns on his next late night out.

At breakfast next morning Louie glanced in the direction of her father, who as good as his word had been up at the crack of dawn and helped with milking the cows. She somehow knew that she would never have cause to hide the guns.

It was the first time she had ever seen him leave food on his plate. Henrietta noticed it and wondered if he was 'coming down with something'; being a heavy sleeper she did not hear him come to bed so knew nothing of the previous night.

"I am going to cycle into Oxford this morning," announced Louie as they rose from the table. Henrietta gave her a puzzled look but said nothing.

"Wrap up warm," said Tom and walked across the hall to his study.

When they were alone in the kitchen Henrietta said, "Do you think you could go to the butcher's in the covered market to get a leg of New Zealand lamb?" Louie's heart sank, she knew she would have plenty to carry but did not tell of her plan.

Tom always insisted on English meat, he had not come to terms with the idea of importing meat, so Henrietta never let him know that she sometimes substituted it, the New Zealand being much less expensive and it being in her nature to economise; she also knew he would not know the difference when it was cooked. Louie mounted her bike and pedalled off towards Oxford.

Now the sun came out and everywhere smelt fresh after the rain. Her spirits rose, she was going to enjoy today, the sheer exhilaration of free wheeling down Headington Hill on to St. Clements and over Magdalen Bridge, down the High Street to Carfax; Tom Tower struck ten o'clock as she swung round into Cornmarket Street, she had made good time.

The delicious aroma of coffee as she neared the Cadena Cafe was irresistible, she would have time for a cup and one of their sticky buns.

The Cadena Cafe was really something, the shop was filled with every confectionery, fresh ground coffee and coffee beans and in the restaurant a balcony went right round the room which was furnished with cane chairs and tables and in the afternoon a small orchestra played and the plates of cream cakes had to be seen to be believed.

Feeling refreshed Louie then made her way to Grimbly Hughes which was almost next door. A fresh-faced young man behind the counter broke off from weighing rice into blue bags, folding down the tops and neatly tying string around the package.

"Good morning Miss, may I be of assistance?" he said very formally.

"Yes please," said Louie, "I would like some of that Stephensons furniture polish which I hear is very good".

"I'm sorry Miss, this is a wholesalers and I don't think I would be allowed to sell you just one bottle".

"Would you be allowed to sell me three dozen?" said Louie. The young man's face lit up, "Oh yes, Miss, but how are you going to carry them?"

"I shall need you to put them into a strong box, I have brought some leather straps to fix them to my carrier".

The young man scratched his head and looked doubtfully at Louie, "I hope you have not got far to go", he said as she settled her bill.

"Not too far" she replied.

And I do hope as you don't fall off with that lot, he thought, as he watched her mount her bike — wobble a bit from the weight — and then pedal off in the direction of the covered market to purchase the New Zealand lamb which fitted into the basket on the handlebars.

It was hard work pushing the bike with all her purchases up Headington Hill but she was quite strong. She had excelled at sport at Lord Williams Grammar School in Thame where she was a boarder; she loved it there except for missing her beloved animals, and especially her father. Her sister Alice and her brothers also attended Lord Williams and she made many friends there.

She reached home tired and hungry just in time for dinner. Dinner was served midday, tea at five o'clock and supper about eight o'clock. She quickly put her bike into the cycle shed and left her furniture cream strapped on the back, the boys were washing their hands at the sink in the scullery. Arthur, pumping water into the hand bowl, turned and smiled at Louie, "Have a good ride?" he asked.

"Yes thanks. How did the hoeing go?" she enquired as she started up the back stairs to change her clothes. "Fine," said Arthur, "we have finished the bottom field."

The boys had been turnip hoeing, they all hated doing that job but their father insisted they took a turn with everything as it is the only way to learn, he used to say. He was a hard task master, but to be fair to him he worked hard himself and in spite of his frequent card playing and hard drinking nights he was a very popular man and had many friends, especially in the farming community. His first wife's father was a veterinary surgeon and had helped and instructed Tom with many animal ailments, so Tom's help was often called upon, sometimes in the middle of the night, with a difficult calving, foaling or lambing and he became quite expert at mixing drenches for all sorts of animal diseases.

The next day they were all gathered round the table for dinner, the vegetable dishes at Henrietta's end piled high with fresh vegetables all from Draycot's very productive garden. There was a dry stone wall round the vegetable garden which sheltered the young plants from strong winds and ensured an early crop — there were bowls of mint sauce and dishes of red currant Jelly. Tom lifted the silver meat cover and proceeded to carve thick slices from the leg of lamb, it was just a tinge underdone in the middle, just how he liked it and the juices ran into the well of the willow patterned dish.

"Well," said Tom when he had eaten a few mouthfuls, "I always say you can't beat a bit of English lamb, those New Zealanders I am darned sure can't rear theirs to taste as good as ours". It was a good thing the boys did not know the truth, Dick would sure to have burst out laughing as they all would have. As it was Henrietta's face went a bit red and she averted her eyes, and Louie doing her best to keep a straight face was secretly making her plans for the afternoon.

As soon as it was possible after dinner she headed for the cycle shed and pedalled swiftly off with her precious cargo in the direction of Worminghall. Her first step was at Mrs. Darvil's lovely big manor house, a maid answered the door and ushered Louie into the spacious drawing room. Mrs. Darvil was sitting in the window seat embroidering an antimacassar; she was delighted to see Louie. They sat and talked for a while, when Mrs. Darvil suggested a cup of tea, Louis begged to be excused as she had some more calls to make. She then told her friend about the furniture polish and was thrilled when she said she would buy two bottles as she had heard it was good and laughingly said it would encourage Mrs Jones, her daily help, though looking round her Louie did not think Mrs. Jones needed much encouragement.

By the end of the afternoon she had made four more calls and sold six bottles. Feeling pleased with her first effort she pedalled home in time for tea.

The next day was butter-making day. Louie loved the clean fresh smell of the dairy and it was always a thrill to feel the butter "come" when turning the handle of the 'end over end' churn; it suddenly had a different feel and sounded 'plompy'. Mater then came and helped to tip it into a big enamel pan and using scales and butter hands (the hands were made of wood, flat on one side and little grooves on the other which made lines on the butter pat) they made it into half and one pound pats, placed them on squares of greased proof paper, most to be sold to regular customers in the village, the rest for the family's consumption.

A month had passed and Louie had made three more trips to Oxford for more furniture polish and then one afternoon her father was in his study writing, "Is that you Louie?" he called as he heard her cross the hall, "I would like a word with you".

He looked very concerned. "What is it father?" asked Louie. "That is what I would like to know" said Tom. "I was at Thame Market yesterday as you know. Old Bill Greenaway came over and had a word with me. He said would I ask you if you could let his missus have some more of the furniture polish you sold her. What did he mean 'sold her', Louie?" Louie knew it was time for explanations, so she told her father about her selling project.

"You see father, I needed some extra money. They have started a tennis club in Thame and I am determined to join but it will cost quite a lot."

"Why didn't you ask me?" said Tom.

"I didn't like to father."

"I admire your initiative my girl," said Tom as he took the key ring from his pocket and opening the bottom drawer of his desk took out a black metal cash box, "but in future you could leave the hawking to the gipsies." He handed her five sovereigns, "and get to your tennis playing, I know how you enjoy it."

"Oh father, I am so looking forward to this summer." Louie got up from the chair.

"Just a minute," said Tom, "I have Bengy coming tomorrow. I thought it was time we had some new pullets and maybe we could sell the old hens to Bengy. I have to go into Thame and since you are into selling things just now, see what you can do with Bengy."

Bengy Brown bought and sold anything from pigs and poultry to dogs and ferrets, whatever you wanted to buy or sell, just ask Bengy.

Louie knew her father had set his heart on getting some Barnevelder hens as they lay a really brown egg. "Mater likes a brown egg," he had said, "and so do I, always tastes better than a white one". *He really would not know the difference if he did not see the shell,* she thought, but she looked forward to seeing the new pullets.

When she saw Bengy ride into the stable yard on his smart little cob, she ran into the dining room and took the whisky decanter from the tantalus and put it beside the teapot. She knew Bengy was partial to a cup of tea and not averse to a drop of the hard stuff.

When she heard his knock she asked Meg to make the tea while she took him down to the chicken run. Meg was the maid who had come to the Lathams on leaving school, she was a happy girl and enjoyed working at Draycot.

Bengy was sitting by the kitchen range sipping tea and enjoying a big wedge of fruit cake. After his second cup, well laced with whisky, he looked at Louie thoughtfully and said, "You know Miss Louie, I don't really want your hens."

"Neither do I Bengy, that's why I am going to sell them to you". She filled his cup for a third time and poured another liberal portion of whisky.

Just as Bengy was leaving through the back door and walking a little unsteadily towards his horse, Tom drove into the yard. He stopped and chatted. "How did you get on with Louie?" he asked after a while, "did she sell you her hens?"

"Miss Louie 'ud sell ice to Eskimos, Mr Latham," said Bengy, "and quite a dab hand at selling furniture polish, I do hear".

"Yes, Bengy, I do hear it too," laughed Tom and hoped he would be safe to ride home. "I'll pick up the chickens tomorrow," said Bengy as he rode out of the gate.

As they went into the dining room, "You managed to sell the hens, Louie?" Tom asked.

"Yes father," said Louie, "I had a bit of a job."

"I see you did," said Tom, glancing at the decanter and chuckling as he sat at the dinner table.

Meg was their only maid now that Alice and Louie had left school and helped around the house. Louie was a very good cook and under Henrietta's guidance soon became adept at the many undertakings of a big farmhouse. She was especially interested in the poultry, whereas Alice did the lighter occupations such as flower arranging and sewing as she liked to keep her hands nice for her piano playing.

She was a very fine pianist and the family would gather in the drawing room in the evenings, the boys scrubbed and changed from their working clothes. They would take turns standing by the piano turning the music sheets for Alice. Henrietta and Louie would be knitting or darning socks and Tom pretending to read 'The Farmer and Stockbreeder' magazine but really revelling in Alice's rendering of the family's favourite tunes: Greensleeves, Linden Lea, To Be a Farmer's Boy and many more.

Greensleeves was Tom's and Louie's favourite. "Supposed to be written by Henry the Eighth," said Tom one evening. "How could such an unpleasant character write such a beautiful tune." Louie nodded agreement. Tom had a very fine baritone voice and would sing the songs he knew and the family would join in the chorus.

TWO

The summer had been enjoyable in every way, weatherwise, as well as everything running smoothly at the farms.

Arthur was courting a nice girl called Blanche, daughter of a neighbouring farmer, and saving hard to get married. Tom liked Blanche and thought she would make Arthur a good wife and had promised him he should have Goldpits Farm when he married. There was a nice little farmhouse which, though not very big as farmhouses go, would make a lovely home. It was situated three fields over with a long drive up to it which was shared with a neighbouring farmer. The worst problem was water, it had to be fetched in milk churns with a horse and cart, though a little thing like that did not daunt the young lovers and they looked forward to having a place of their own and getting married.

Alice had met George Graham at a party, he was quite a lot older than Alice and sadly was blind, their musical interests drew them together and it soon became obvious that they were in love. When he proposed to her Alice unhesitatingly accepted even though she knew he wanted her to go with him to live in San Francisco. It was a great shock to the family. They were married in the village Church and a week later set sail to start a new life on distant shores.

It was a lovely wedding. Alice wore a smart blue suit and carried a bouquet of roses. George gently touched the soft petals and smelt their intoxicating perfume. Tom had insisted on having a marquee. There were eight men working on the three farms besides the family, they and their wives were invited and very many friends and neighbours.

Louie and Henrietta revelled in arranging the catering and Meg was beside herself with excitement, all went well and apart from being tinged with sadness at the impending parting it was a day to remember.

When the day of departure came it was all Alice could do not to change her mind, but with all her possessions packed and sent in advance to the docks and the sight of her husband helplessly waiting for her to guide him on to the train she hugged her family in turn and with tears streaming down her face she led her George into the carriage. Louie was devastated and when the train had steamed out of sight she hurried to the trap which was waiting in the station yard. No-one spoke a word on the journey home, it was fairly certain they would never see Alice again.

When Louie took a cup of tea to her father, who was sitting alone in his study, his eyes were moist and his hand shook as he took the cup and saucer. "She was very brave," he said without looking up.

"I'm sure she will be alright father," Louie said.

There were five horses besides the ones used for the farm work; the boys had one each, they were fine horsemen, especially Lambourn. There was Gladys, the mare used for pulling the trap and a cob called Cob-nut which was used mostly in the milk float to take the churns of milk to the station.

After his old hunter died Tom took to just using the trap. Louie, though loving the horses, when not using the trap was happy to pedal her trusty old bike.

Once a week she would drive Henrietta into Thame to do the shopping, she looked forward to this and it never failed to thrill her to take the reins as Gladys would trot briskly down the country lanes. She was a very fine horse and Tom was particularly fond and proud of her, she was bright chestnut with a white blaze and white stockings, she had kind eyes and nature and when Tom had spent an evening having a "few bevies" Gladys would always get him home. How she manipulated the trap through the gateway was speculated upon by all and sundry but she always managed.

It was a nice sunny morning early in June. Arthur and Dick had gone to Tetsworth after breakfast to work at Goldpits, Lambourn was doing some fencing in the front field. Tom came down the stairs followed by Henrietta, both dressed for going out.

Tom had been very low and depressed since Alice's departure and Louie and Henrietta had conspired to take him out of himself for a day. It was decided Henrietta was in need of a new dress and persuaded him to take her into Oxford.

Louie had a tennis match arranged for the evening so she was tidying up the herbacious border. Jessy was standing at the horse's head talking quietly to Gladys and stroking her neck, Tom helped Henrietta into the trap and as he climbed in and took the reins, he said to Jessy, "When you have finished in the stables perhaps you could give Lambourn a hand with the fencing my boy". Tom called all his men 'my boy' even when they were quite old. Jessy was twenty-five but looked younger.

He touched his cap, nodded, and went whistling off towards the stables. He liked Lambourn and was looking forward to his day.

Louie felt she had made a good job of her weeding and went into the house to see how Meg was getting on with sweeping and dusting in the big panelled dining room. "I think refreshment is the order of the day," she said, heading for the kitchen. Meg gathered up her dustpan and brush and duster, glanced round with satisfaction and followed. They were just sitting down to enjoy a mug of cocoa and a doorstep of bread with thick slices of cheese when there was the sound of running footsteps up the path to the back door and the latch being lifted. There stood Lambourn gasping for breath and as white as a sheet. "Louie come quick, I have had an accident." Louie and Meg leapt to their feet and followed him across the field. Jessy was sitting on the bank on Lambourn's coat with blood pouring from his hand.

"It weren't master Lam's fault, Miss Louie," he said. "My hand just got in the way, he hit it with the sledge hammer when he were driving in the post," then he passed out.

"We must get him to hospital as quickly as we can," Louie said to Lambourn when she had sent Meg running to the house for some clean sheeting to wrap the injured hand, and some blankets. "Father won't be back for ages with the trap so it will have to be the milk float. Go and start harnessing Cob-nut, I will come and help as soon as Meg gets back here". By the time they had wrapped up Jessy and swathed his hand in sheeting and Louie — leaving Meg with the still unconscious Jessy — had reached the stable yard, Lambourn was fastening the final buckles on the harness. Louie grabbed bundies of hay and threw them into the bottom of the cart and they drove back across the field to where Jessy lay. They made him as comfortable as possible with the hay and blankets and carefully lifted him into the cart. Meg sat beside him still in her working apron. After stopping to leave a note for whoever of the family came home first they headed for the hospital as fast as the old horse could go.

It seemed an endless journey, especially as Jessy had regained consciousness and was moaning with pain. For some time Louie had wondered if Meg had fallen in love with Jessy and her suspicion was confirmed when she saw Meg's anguished face. When they reached the hospital a nursing sister took charge and a doctor was soon on the spot, the sister smiled kindly at the dishevelled trio and told them they could come back in the morning and see how he was. "He is in good hands," she assured them, so they climbed aboard the milk float and allowing the old cob a little more leisurely pace made their way back, calling on Jessy's mother, Mrs. Grant, to tell her what had happened.

Mrs. Grant was a widow, her husband had been killed when Jessy was a baby. He had worked on the railway and was hit by a train, and Flora Grant brought the lad up, she took in washing as well as "charing" which was mostly scrubbing floors and sweeping and dusting and took Jessy with her, but he was a good little boy and nobody minded him running round while his mother was working. She worked three days a week at Draycot so when

Jessy came to work there it was a natural progression, he fitted in well and everyone liked him.

"Now do come in and have a cup of tea," she said when they stopped at her cottage and told her what had happened, "you look all in". Though they were anxious to get home they gratefully accepted and after arranging to pick up Mrs. Grant in the morning to take her to see Jessy they made their way back to the farm.

Tom and Henrietta had very much enjoyed their trip to Oxford. They had done their shopping in the morning, purchasing a very nice dress for Henrietta and a fancy waistcoat for Tom, they had lunch at the Mitre Hotel and as it was such a lovely day they took a stroll down the High Street as far as Magdalen Bridge. They walked through the Botanical Gardens and watched the Mallard on the river, there was a Moorhen's nest near the far bank resting precariously on a cluster of sticks and they could just see the speckled eggs.

Henrietta was pleased to see Tom looking so relaxed and happy. They walked through the lovely gardens and down beside the river and through Christ Church Meadows. Going back through the covered market they bought fruit and fresh herrings to take back for supper.

When they got home and heard about Jessy it rather put a damper on the day. After supper, Tom suggested an early night and resolved to get up extra early in the morning to get the milking done, he was anxious to get to the hospital as soon as possible.

Next morning Lambourn, like his father, was up extra early, he still felt responsible for what had happened. He said he would ride into Thame on his horse as it needed shoeing and it would leave more room in the trap as Louie had asked if Meg may accompany them.

By half past eight, milking done and breakfasted, Tom, Louie and Meg set out in the trap, to first pick up Flora Grant and then away to Thame to the Cottage Hospital.

Lambourn met them at the Hospital entrance after leaving his horse at the blacksmith's shop. They were ushered into the

Matron's office by a pretty little nurse, the Matron was sitting by the window at a very big desk. She was about to give the verdict on Jessy's injuries when there was a tap at the door and a doctor came in. He recognised Louie at once as he was a member of the tennis club and had once or twice partnered Louie in the mixed doubles.

After brief introductions and pleasantries he proceeded to tell them about Jessy. "The good news is we hope we have saved his fingers. They will take a while to mend and he will be in hospital for a week or two." Flora was glad she had brought his pyjamas and dressing gown and Louie was thinking he may be pleased with the fresh eggs, fruit and flowers she had hurriedly packed at the last minute. "Now," said the doctor, looking serious, "something has happened which I think I should tell you before you see the patient so that you can be prepared. You see his hair turned white overnight, it happens very occasionally with shock. We have told him, he is still a bit weak though and has not said very much so I don't know if he has taken it in."

They were allowed to visit only for a few minutes two at a time. Lambourn was last to go in on his own. Jessy looked at Lambourn and knowing how he was feeling gave a reassuring little chuckle, "I look a funny old young bugger don't I, Master Lam?"

Lambourn smiled and patted his shoulder. "Well hurry up and get better old, young bugger," he said, "we've still got that b..... fence to finish."

On the way home, everyone was rather subdued, then Tom said, "Will you be alright on your own, Flora?"

"Yes thank you, sir" she said. "Jess will have his wages in full," said Tom, "and we shall take you in to see him as often as possible".

"That is a relief to me," said Flora. "I were wondering how we were going to manage. Jess is a fair old trencherman and will want a bit of building up when he gets home." Tom and Louie reassured her and told her not to worry on that score.

They dropped her at her pretty little cottage and headed for Draycot. Just before they reached home Meg, who had been very quiet, looked up and said so seriously, "Well white hair or not I do still luv un." She looked at Tom, "Mind you he don't know it".

"I wouldn't bet on that," said Tom, "he is not as green as he's cabbage looking as the saying goes".

"I would not say he is exactly cabbage-looking at the moment, sir, more like a cauliflower I reckon", said Meg. They all laughed then, not unkindly as they knew Jess would have enjoyed the comparison and never minded a bit of mickey taking.

Tom flicked the reins and Gladys trotted on sharply, Lambourn had reached home before them, knowing some bridle paths which cut short his journey and was telling the family how Jessy was faring.

THREE

Six months had passed since Jessy's accident, his hand had healed remarkably well, his hair was still snowy white and though it was speculated on when he first came out of hospital everyone had got used to seeing it.

Arthur had married his Blanche and they were now living at Goldpits Farm. After a quiet wedding, which was their wish and a short honeymoon, they were delighted to be back and fulfilling their ambitions of running their very own farm. Arthur working on the farm and Blanche getting the house and garden into shape. It was a nice house and was responding to her loving care, even with the "usual offices" of the day, namely a bucket "lavvy" down the bottom of the garden and a tin bath in the wash-house, it was home and they loved it.

Each day Arthur would take the horse and cart and drive two miles to fill milk churns with water, there was a rain water butt to catch the water from the roof which was a bonus.

The family were sitting round the fire in the drawing room at Draycot, Tom enjoying a last pipe of tobacco before retiring to bed said solemnly, "I have been thinking, would you consider it would be a good idea if we went to live at Harlesford Farm?" The family, a little stunned at first, all agreed that it would, the house would be easier to run and more suitable for the diminishing family. Another reason, Tom pointed out, there was a nice cottage quite near to the house and if Meg and Jessy agreed to live there when they married Meg could still help in the house part time.

They were thrilled when told of the new plans and arranged for the wedding to coincide with the move. Flora, though sad to lose Jessy was pleased he had chosen Meg, she had always liked her and felt sure they would be well suited. "He's a sensible lad," she thought, "they'll do."

Louie was still enjoying her tennis playing and had made many new friends, the Hospital doctor in particular, James Harding. There was no doubt about his feelings for Louie and he got on well with all the family and now spent much of his spare time at Harlesford.

"You are seeing a lot of James, Louie," said Tom one evening when they were alone in the garden. They were sitting in deck chairs under a weeping willow tree, Tom sucking his pipe and Louie reading her favourite poetry book, now and then reading aloud a poem that she felt her father would enjoy.

"Yes, father" she said, "I am very fond of James."

"I thought you were sweet on Algy," said Tom. Algernon Hutt was a farmer's son from nearby Wheatfield, he was the youngest of nine children and was two years older than Louie. They had known each other from childhood as their families had always been friends.

"So I am father, but if you are trying to marry me off you are out of luck, I am not in any hurry."

"You are going to search the orchard and pick a crabapple at last" laughed Tom.

"I'm not searching really, just enjoying life," she replied. "I think it is time we went in, even your stinky old pipe does not keep the midges away." The next day was Sunday and the family had been invited to Wheatfield for the day. James was on duty at the hospital so would not be coming to Harlesford.

Henrietta, Louie and Tom went in the trap and Lambourn and Dick on horseback as they would probably join Algy and Reggie for a ride round the farm in the afternoon. It was a model farm. Like Tom, Edwin Hutt was a first rate farmer and they had lots to discuss. On the journey Tom would now and then stop Gladys to peep over the hedge to see how Edwin's crops were coming along.

The sound of horses' hooves on the gravel drive brought the

Hutt family out to welcome their friends. Edwin's wife had died three years previously, and Kate being the eldest had assumed the roll of hostess. She loved cooking and was never happier than preparing something special when friends visited and this meal was no exception. Edwin and Tom then went into the sitting room with cigars and brandy and the womenfolk headed for the drawing room for a tete-a-tete.

Besides Kate there was Emily, Sara, Anne, Ida, Minnie and Lizzie. They were a jolly crowd and Louie was looking forward to hearing all their news but as they were crossing the hall Algy waylaid her and asked if she would come for a walk. "Kate needs some watercress for supper," he said, "so shall we go to the cressbeds?"

They were walking across the meadow arm in arm when Edwin and Tom spotted them from the window, "I would like to think they will marry some day," said Tom. "Nothing would please me more," replied Edwin, "but what about James?"

"They are fond of each other there is no denying," said Tom and tomorrow Louie is going to Derbyshire to stay with his people while he is on vacation."

Algy and Louie had reached the brook and were wading in barefoot to pick the watercress. As Algy bent over and concentrated on selecting the best cress, Louie gave him a playful push from behind. He lost his balance and fell headlong into the water.

"Well, I think my money is on James," said Edwin as they watched Louie pick up her long skirt and run for home. Algy in hot pursuit soon caught her up and when they saw them kissing the two men smiled, "perhaps fifty-fifty," said Tom. "Time will tell."

"I want to tell you about a plan I have," said Edwin. "For some time now I have toyed with the idea of buying a motor car, the family keep dropping hints about how useful it would be. I know I said I would never have one, but it is a changing world Tom, and I have decided to see about getting one next week."

Tom, having smoked his cigar was filling his old pipe with tobacco. "Would you mind if I came with you, Edwin? I have been thinking about getting one for some time but have put it off until I talked to you, but you have convinced me now."

While Louie and James were in Derbyshire, Algy had a serious talk with his father. "I think I shall lose Louie, if I haven't already," he said. Edwin agreed and after a long discussion it was settled that Algy should visit the bank manager the very next day. "We will take the car," said Edwin. "You need some practice with your driving. I have some shopping to do. Tell Mr. Hudson I will stand surety for you."

Mr. Hudson, the bank manager, had known Edwin and his family for years and he and his wife had enjoyed visiting them at Wheatfield. He liked Algy and knew he was a hard-working young man and finally agreed to help him with finance if he could find the right farm to rent.

Algy's head was in a whirl, supposing Louie would not marry him, supposing she was already promised to James, he had taken it for granted that she would be his wife some day, but he had not bargained for James to appear on the scene. He had striven for years and saved for a farm of his own. Louie had always figured in his plans.

Louie and James spent a wonderful fortnight at his home. His parents and sister were charming, it was evident they idolised James and his father was pleased and proud that he had followed his profession — he was a surgeon but had recently retired.

They explored the highways and byways, sometimes on foot and sometimes in James's father's car which had a nasty habit of breaking down and it was a case of 'get out and get under,' or 'get out and push,' so James, not being very mechanically minded often opted for the pony and trap.

On further acquaintance with James's family, Louie realised that James must have indicated that he intended marrying her which made her feel a little bewildered as she was not sure of her feelings for him. She knew she was very fond of him, but found herself comparing him with Algy, big strong Algy with his blue eyes and red hair. James was slender and tall with gentle expressive brown eyes. James, whose life was dedicated to helping others and like his father, took his profession very seriously.

As the days passed, Louie was thinking more and more about home and in spite of the wonderful hospitality and the fact that she was so enjoying being with James she found herself wondering how her pet lambs were faring. Each year she reared the orphaned lambs, bottle feeding them until they were old enough to be returned to the flock. She wondered if the broody hen had hatched the clutch of turkey eggs; she had left instructions about feeding the baby turkey chicks when they hatched. She thought about the dogs, especially Skip her terrier and wondered if he was missing her.

When the day came for their return, Louie found it difficult to contain her excitement — she did not want anyone to know she was feeling homesick, especially the Harding family. She did not fool James but he kept his own counsel and gave no indication that he had guessed her secret. In fact in a way he was pleased to be returning himself, wondering how his patients were progressing and taking small gifts for the sick children in his care at the hospital.

While Louie was away Tom had ordered a telephone to be installed at Harlesford. Edwin and he had put in their applications together, it was such a novelty and at first Henrietta refused to lift the receiver when the bell rang. "I shall not touch the confounded thing," she said but when she heard Tom speaking to Edwin she plucked up courage and asked if she could have a word with Kate. When she heard Kate's apprehensive, "hello," she couldn't believe her ears and promptly forgot what she was going to say.

"Give it here girl," said Edwin and took the instrument from her shaking hand, while he explained to Kate that Henrietta would ring her when she was more used to the telephone. Henrietta sank down in the nearest chair. "Well I never did," she murmured, but resolved to try again when she was more composed.

Almost as soon as she was back, Louie received a 'phone call from Algy. It was the first time either of them had spoken on the telephone and there was much hesitating and giggling. Algy told her that his father had allowed him to borrow the car and would she come for a ride in it tomorrow. Louie agreed, wondering where they would go. "I'll be there early," he had said and sure enough at just gone nine Edwin's beautiful new car came slowly up the drive at Harlesford with Algy at the wheel, a smart new Harris Tweed jacket and matching cap and broad grin.

"Come on in," said Tom. "Louie won't be long, she has been helping Henrietta with the butter." At that moment Louie came bounding down the stairs looking radiant in a floral summer dress and carrying a cardigan.

"You had better bring a coat" said Algy, "though it looks like being a nice day."

They were soon bowling along towards Oxford, Algy drove slowly through the city and Louie had to admire the way he had mastered the controls in so short a time. They had reached the top of Cumnor Hill heading for Faringdon before he tentatively asked if she had enjoyed her holiday, hoping against hope that she had not made any promises to James.

Her reply was pretty negative. If she had enjoyed it she did not give any indication one way or the other, just telling him about some of the places she had visited. By this time they had nearly reached a village called Eaton Hastings and Algy turned the car into a lane leading to a field gate. He has been here before thought Louie as he pulled the car up beside the gate. They walked arm in arm across three meadows and then through a spinney. "Are we trespassing?" asked Louie. "There does not seem to be a footpath here."

"No there isn't," he replied "but we are not trespassing."

When they returned to the car Algy reached in the back and took out a picnic basket. "Come on", he said, "I have something to show you." They walked back up the lane until they reached the road, then on the opposite side down another lane. There they stopped and gazed at the panorama before them, there was a lake with tall trees surrounding it and in the trees were dozens of large untidy nests.

Louie had never seen a heronry before, she had seen herons flying over Draycot and Harlesford and fishing in the streams but never so many together, their long legs hanging out of the nests.

They stood for some time just watching those beautiful birds and taking in the magic of the scene, then Algy led Louie to a fallen tree where they sat down. He opened the picnic basket, "the girls packed this for us, under Kate's supervision, of course." They were both hungry and did justice to the lovely spread after which they lay down on the grass in the warm sunshine.

"Louie," said Algy, do you like it here?"

"Its Heaven," she said drowsily, the long walk, the food and the warm sunshine coupled with the fact that she had been up early, was making her feel sleepy. "Will you marry me and come here to live?"

Louie sat bolt upright. "You are joking of course?"

"I have never been so serious in my life," said Algy. "The farm we have just walked round is to let, it belongs to Lord Faringdon and he will build a farmhouse for the tenant — he has given me first refusal".

"We could become engaged until the house is built," he said.

Louie fell silent. Was she ready for marriage? She supposed she should be, she was nearly twenty-six. She thought of Henrietta and Tom. How would they manage? *Well they have managed for a fortnight so I am not indispensable.*

She thought about James, dear James, how would she tell him, but most importantly how could she refuse Algy. In her heart she knew it was he that she loved. She also knew she was not cut out to be a doctor's wife, the farming way of life was in her blood and she could not imagine living in any other environment. She also knew that life with Algy would not be a 'bed of roses', his hot-headed ways and bad temper were well known. Louie had never seen that side of him but knew only too well it existed.

"We could stop in Oxford on the way back and choose a ring," his arm was round her and he hugged her close to him.

"We would need capital to stock the farm and implements — have you thought this out?" she said. He told her about the visit to the bank manager and the amount he had saved.

There did not seem to be any more obstacles and finally Louie agreed to marry him as soon as the house was built at Kilminsters Farm.

On the return journey Louie wondered how the family would receive her news. They had reached Oxford and Algy stopped the car in the High Street, determined to buy the ring that very day and though Louie protested that they would have so many ways for their money to be spent, he insisted on a very beautiful ring with three diamonds set in a gold band. When they reached Harlesford the reception to their news was mixed. Tom was delighted, he had always hoped for this union. Lambourn and Dick hugged her in turn and wished her happiness, but Henrietta had difficulty in disguising her disappointment — she had hoped that Louie would marry James but she kissed them both and hurried from the room on the pretext of helping Meg bring in the tea.

The weeks flew by, there was so much to do. Louie preparing her bottom drawer, collecting table and bed linen and Algy going to farm sales to buy farm machinery and tools.

They made several trips to Eaton Hastings. Lord Faringdon arranged to meet them at Kilminsters Farm to decide on the position of the house and the size and number of rooms.

"He is such a nice man," Louie told Henrietta, "not a bit like I imagined a Lord to be."

On each trip they visited the Heronry, noting the progress of the young herons and when some had left the nests and were attempting to fly. They lost all sense of time as they watched them and had to light lamps on the car before reaching home. Their excuse for being so late was not entirely believed by the family who were getting anxious and wondering if the car had broken down.

James still spent most of his off-duty time at Harlesford. When Louie told him she had become engaged to Algy he took her into his arms. "Why do you think I have never proposed to you"? he said. "For one thing I knew you were in love with him and another thing he is bigger than me if it came to a contest!" They laughed and kissed and promised each other they would always be friends.

CHAPTER 4

The war was imminent, the posters with Lord Kitchener pointing his finger and saying 'Your Country Needs You' were everywhere. Lambourn and Dick were enjoying a drink at the local. The conversation in the saloon was predominantly about the inevitable approach of a war with Germany. Their companion, Henry Adams, was the only son of a neighbouring farmer and he told them he was going to join the New Zealanders.

"The sooner we get in the sooner it will be over," he said.

"How is your Dad going to manage?" asked Lambourn.

"I have not told him yet, they may not accept me and it won't be for long."

Henry looked at Dick "What about coming with me, Dick, we would have those Germans licked in no time flat."

Dick looked thoughtful. "I will let you know Henry," he said. "I will have to talk it over with Father". When they reached home Dick and Lambourn sat smoking their pipes and talking until far into the night. Lambourn was engaged to Edie Blay and as Dick was 'foot loose and fancy free' if anyone went they finally agreed it would be him.

The next evening after supper Tom and Dick went for a walk to the bottom meadow to check on the sheep and a cow that was near to calving. Dick told his father about Henry going to enrol in the army and his suggestion that he go with him. Tom's heart sank, he knew that whatever he said, Dick would make up his own mind and do what his conscience told him he must do. He felt sympathy for his neighbour Geoff Adams. Henry practically ran the farm now Geoff was 'getting the rheumatics'. *I suppose if he can manage so can I,* thought Tom, but the thing uppermost in his mind were the dangers and horrors that inevitably would face his beloved youngest son.

Dick smiled reassuringly at his father. "Anyway, I bet you a pound to a penny it will be over before I have finished my training," he said. "Don't tell the womenfolk yet Dick, the army may not need you". Though even as he said it he was pretty sure the army would need him and many thousands like him before long.

Kilminsters Farm house was nearly completed and the date had been set for Louie and Algy's wedding. It was brought forward so that Dick could attend before he was drafted overseas. He had nearly finished his training. He and Henry had so far stayed in the same unit and their overseas posting had come together.

So much for Dick's prediction that the war would be over thought Tom, contrary to everyone's hopes, there was no end in sight. Tom and Geoff had become closer friends in their joint anxiety and Tom would often send one of his men over to help Geoff with sheep shearing or hay-making, though without Dick he was hard pressed himself to keep the farm running smoothly. He was also dreading the thought of Louie leaving Harlesford, but at least she will not be very far away, he thought, not like Alice, such a long way away. Her letters were full of glowing accounts of her new environment but Tom could detect a certain sadness and wondered if she was still a little homesick.

It was a quiet wedding, just family and a few close friends and the reception at Harlesford. Louie wondered if James would accept his invitation. How would she feel if the situation were reversed, but he did come and was the first to kiss the bride. Later at the reception he had a quiet word with Louie and told her he would be joining the army. "They desperately need doctors at the front," he said. Louie promised to write to him and made him promise to visit them at Kilminsters Farm on his leaves. She knew he would be sure to make Harlesford his first 'port of call'; it was like a second home to him now. They took a stroll down the garden, it was the first of May and the spring flowers were blooming in spite of it being a cold late late spring, but today the sun was shining. This should be the happiest day of my life thought Louie but how can it be with both Dick and James off to the front?

They did not have a honeymoon as there was so much to do at Kilminsters Farm and they were both eager to get into their lovely new house. Algy promised that when the harvest was in they would go away for a few days.

One of the first neighbours to befriend them was Charlie Norman. He lived at Buscot in a beautiful old farmhouse on the banks of the River Thames. Just beyond the house was a weir and the water splashing over it was awe-inspiring. Charlie was a hard-working young farmer, he had a club foot and in spite of his specially made boots he walked with a limp. He was kindness itself and helped Louie and Algy in many ways. He found them a carter and a cowman who were real characters but Charlie assured them they would be good workers. "Now Louie, if you can persuade Grace Wheeler to come and char for you, you would have a treasure, but she is funny about who she works for and if she does not take to you she will not come."

Grace Wheeler lived in the middle of Buscot in a stone semi-detached cottage. There was a stone outhouse in the garden and when Louie went up the path, facing her the length of the outhouse were strings and strings of onions, the biggest she had ever seen. She tapped a little nervously on the front door, it was opened by a tall woman with a round face and laughing eyes, she was wearing a sacking apron, high button up boots and a man's cap on backwards.

"Come in, ma'am," she said when Louie had introduced herself and she was shown into a spotless little parlour. The windowsill was full of geraniums and a kettle was singing on the hob.

Over a cup of tea the deal was struck and Grace Wheeler agreed to come each morning, except Sundays, to Kilminsters "and give you a do through. I'll start tomorrow," she said decisively. Grace proudly presented Louie with a basket of onions to take home. "We will never eat this lot and my Bert do love growing them," she said. As they didn't have a garden yet, Louie was pleased to accept them.

Bert was Charlie's cowman, "a man in a million", Charlie described him, and "Grace is a woman in a million, I am pleased she is going to work for Louie".

"Louie was quite taken with her headgear," said Algy. "Oh the cap — I have never seen her without it. I once asked Bert if she wears it in bed." He said, "I be too tired to notice what she wears when I gets to bed master, but I 'udn't be surprised and it is always backwards so's the peak don't get in the way when I kisses her."

"He is a card," said Charlie, "but you will like the folk hereabouts". Algy reckoned he would and accepted Charlie's invitation to go fishing with him that evening. "There is a big old spotted trout lies just under the weir, I have been after him for weeks now but he is too wily for me, you try your luck. He would be supper enough for two if you can catch him!"

"I have not done much fishing," admitted Algy, "never had much time."

"Perhaps you will have beginner's luck then," said Charlie.

They telephoned Louie to say they would be late, armed themselves with fishing tackle and set off towards the weir. That evening cemented a friendship that was to last for many years and resulted in Algy becoming hooked on fishing. Just sitting quietly on the river bank and watching the wild life was enjoyment enough without the added anticipation of a catch. They landed three nice trout and decided to call it a day as both men had to be up early next morning to milk the cows. Once more Wily Willy, as Charlie called the big trout, had eluded them. They packed their catch for Algy to take home and Charlie agreed to go to Kilminsters for supper the next evening.

It had been a good summer after the cold wet start and the haymaking was a success, as was the harvest. 'A dripping June puts all things in tune,' thought Algy as he proudly watched the thatchers at work thatching the ricks. Before balers were invented the hay was put loose into ricks with elevators which sent the hay up on a sort of spiked conveyor belt and dropped it into the middle of the rick. There were usually two people on the rick with hay forks, one to pass the hay out to the rick builder who made it into a square or oblong shape; the corn ricks were often round. There was a special tool to cut the hay out in wedges about a yard or metre square. Often the rick would heat in the middle, especially if the hay had not dried out enough and a long iron bar was pushed into the rick to test the heat of it. Many a sleepless night farmers had in case their ricks caught fire.

Louie was making plans for their first 'harvest home', it was traditional to have a party for the workers and their families, neighbouring farmers and friends turned up too to join in the festivities.

Dick was home from France and planning to spend the last week of his leave at Kilminsters so the harvest home was arranged to coincide with his stay. "He's in a poor old way," Henrietta told Louie when they were discussing the arrangements on the telephone, "anything you can do to cheer him up has got to be good". His friend Henry could not come home as he was in hospital, a bit of shrapnel had hit him in the leg. They were side by side when it happened and Dick had half carried him across 'no-man's land' to an ambulance. He made light of the incident not wanting to let the parents know just what hell it was to be fighting in a war that was to end all wars. Henry's father, Geoff, came and spent the day at Harlesford. He talked non-stop to Dick to glean information about Henry, letters from the troops in the trenches were few and far between.

Dick noted a great change in Geoff and knew life for him was far from easy. He was determined to keep the farm in good fettle for Henry to come back to and as the war dragged on all farmers were pressed to the limit to supply food for the nation. Dick was careful not to even hint of the horrors they were enduring but no one was fooled, least of all Geoff. The happy-go-lucky, carefree fellow who stepped on the train with his Henry and went off full of optimism had changed so very much. Geoff fell to wondering what it had done to his son and longed to see him.

The arrival of Dick at Kilminsters aroused mixed feelings in Louie and Algy. They were so pleased to see him but tried not to show the shock they had at his appearance.

The harvest home had been planned for three days' time and they were making preparations, Algy arranging trestle tables in the stone barn and Louie with the help of Grace, cooking farmhouse fare. Dick was soon roped in to help. "It's taking him out of himself," said Grace. "That is what he needs and plenty of good food and he will get that here for sure."

"What would you say if we made a meal of the tom turkey while Dick is here," said Algy. "A good idea," said Louie, "but it could be a little celebration."

"Louie, you don't mean....,"

"I could be, but it is early days," she said.

"It will be a boy," said Algy after kissing her and rushing out to tell Dick and Grace.

The day for Dick to go back came all too soon and meant an early start for him to catch the milk train to London. Algy would not hear of his suggestion that he go in the milk float. They would all go in the trap. "We have had such a good harvest we may be able to afford a car by your next visit," he said. Dick came into the kitchen to find Louie making sandwiches for his journey. "Steady on Louie, there is only one of me and there is enough there to feed a battalion," he said as she continued to put slices of home-cured ham between bread that had come out of the oven that very morning. "You must have been up all night" he said.

"I am very happy for you both and am really looking forward to being an uncle. Make sure it is a boy, Louie, Algy has so set his heart on it".

He stooped and stroked Skip lying on the hearthrug, "I would give the world to change places with dear old Skip but I could not wish on a dog the life I shall be returning to." When he looked up and saw Louie's face he regretted his words and hastened to add, "I think it will soon be over now though."

The afternoon after Dick's departure Louie walked up to the heronry and said a silent prayer for his safety. She thought that if God was listening he would hear her from this peaceful spot, but he could not have been listening as three weeks later the dreaded telegram came to Harlesford from the War Office to say Dick had been killed in action.

Trouble never comes singly and a week later fate struck another blow. Louie was wakened with gravel being thrown at the bedroom window. She shook Algy who was a heavy sleeper and was out of bed in a flash.

"Master Hutt do come down quick, the ricks be afire!" It was Sid the cowman with his trousers pulled on over his night shirt. "Jake be on his way but I don't think as there's a dang thing we can do." One look told Algy there was undoubtedly nothing they could do, it had got a real hold and the balmy night with a gentle breeze did nothing to discourage it.

Louie had rushed to the 'phone and was waiting impatiently for the postmistress to answer before she could be put through to the fire brigade. By the time they arrived the rick yard was well alight and despite their efforts, by the dawn there was precious little left of their first harvest, just heaps of smoking black ash to show for a year's hard labour.

Thankfully no animals were involved as the cattle sheds and pig sties were situated well away from the rick yard but Algy's first thoughts were how he was going to feed his stock this winter and with no corn to sell, how was he going to pay the rent.

The next afternoon a waggon came up the drive piled high with hay.

Algy recognised one of Charlie's men leading the big shire horse. "The Boss sent this to tide you over." Louie had come out and he put his arm around her. She pretended not to notice the tear, they went in together to phone Charlie. "The best friend a man ever had," he said.

Michaelmas Day was fast approaching, the day for paying the rent, and Louie knew that Algy was having sleepless nights. Edwin was not a well man and though Algy knew he would help him he was loathe to ask him and did not let him know the extent of the devastation in his rick yard. They did not let Tom know either in case he told Edwin.

It was a typically hot sultry September afternoon. Louie took a basket and went in search of blackberries. After picking for about an hour she headed for the heronry vaguely hoping that the peace and beauty of the place would inspire her to think of a way out of their predicament. She sat on her favourite log and put her head in her hands, worry and the fact that the baby was due in about three weeks all contributed to her feeling of exhaustion. No inspiration came and just as she decided to go home and get Algy's tea she felt a hand on her shoulder. She had been so deep in thought she had not heard the approaching footsteps. Startled, she tried to jump up, but the pressure on her shoulder intensified, then to her great relief a voice that she knew.

"I did not mean to startle you, Louie, but I was on my way to Kilminsters when I saw you sitting there. I have only just got back from Scotland and heard the news of Dick's death". It was Lord Faringdon, he sat beside her on the log. "Did he tell you I met him at this very spot just before he went back. We had a long talk, I liked him very much."

After voicing his condolences he brought up the matter of the fire. "Do you know how it started?" he said.

"We have no idea your Lordship," said Louie, "we are sure it was not a hot rick of hay and Algy is very strict about the men smoking. We wondered if it was a tramp — they sleep in rickyards as you know."

"Well, if I may, I will come back with you, I want a word with Algy." Louie's heart sank. *I bet he is going to ask him for the rent,* she thought, but he went on, "I have an idea about the rent I want to put to him and I am dying for a cup of tea." He smiled at her.

"Algy is a very proud man, Sir".

"I know that, Louie, don't worry," he said, taking her arm as they walked towards Kilminsters. They talked about the baby and he told Louie about his family. When they reached the rickyard gate he looked with dismay at the blackened earth, "I really am very sorry," he said, and Louie knew her first impression of him was right, he was a real gentleman.

She was glad she had made fresh scones that morning and by the time Algy came in from milking the cows the tea was ready and they discussed his Lordship's plan. He suggested that they forgo this year's rent but make it up in future years as they could afford it. Algy was so relieved words failed him.

Lord Faringdon smiled at Louie. "I said it would be alright."

The first baby to be born at Kilminsters was indeed a boy, though it must be said he was a delicate little fellow, so frail and puny that young Dr. Pullen advised an early christening. Louie would have liked to call him Dick but after much discussion and seeing the pleasure it had given Edwin to see his first grandchild, knowing how frail he had become and the store he had set on it being a boy to carry on the family name, they finally decided to call him Edwin Algernon.

Dr. Pullen made frequent calls as he was not happy with little Edwin's progress. When he was about a fortnight old he discovered that the little chap had a rupture and would need an operation. "He is so very young," protested Louie.

They took him into Oxford the next day and left him at the Ackland Home Hospital knowing he was in good hands but loathe to part with their little treasure. All went well however, and he was soon restored to them.

The strain was beginning to tell, especially on Algy and when Charlie suggested a day's fishing Louie was pleased when he accepted. She packed a hamper of food and a bottle of her good elderberry wine. After milking the cows he dressed up warmly and as there had been a lot of rain he put on some thick woollen socks and hob-nailed boots.

Jake brought the trap round to the front door as they were saying goodbye to Louie and as they watched the horse trotting off up the drive Jake said, "That will do the master good, ma'am, he has been like a bear with a sore head lately what with the fire and the babby being so poorly."

"I'm sure it will," said Louie, "he does enjoy his fishing and he has not had much chance lately."

When Algy arrived at Buscot, Charlie was waiting with the fishing tackle and they were soon trudging off, carrying the hamper between them, towards the upper reaches above the weir. "I saw Wily Willy yesterday," said Charlie. "I wonder if it will be our lucky day".

The two friends settled down to their fishing. The river was very fast-flowing with the recent rains and Algy wondered if it was better for fishing that way. He soon had a bite, it was a small pike which he popped back into the water. They opened the hamper and really enjoyed their meal, polishing off Louie's elderberry wine. After a pipe of tobacco and chatting a while they went back to their fishing.

After about half an hour Algy had a bite and he knew it was a big fish. "I think I have caught old Willy," he shouted to Charlie who was soon by his side. There was no doubt it was the big trout and he took some landing. The two men looked in admiration at the beautiful silvery fish.

"Shall we give him another chance?" said Algy, slipping out the hook. Charlie nodded, fishing would not be the same without him.

Algy picked up the trout in his arms and walked to the edge of the river, as he bent forward to drop him in the water the fish gave a wriggle and he lost his footing and slipped down the bank into the river, the wily fish flicked his tail and swam away but Algy, unfortunately, could not swim. Even if he had been able to, with his heavy boots and the strong current he would have been hard put to save himself. He looked aghast at Charlie and next minute was under water being swept towards the weir. Charlie looked transfixed wondering whether to go for help. He could not swim so it was no use trying to rescue his friend, there was a lifebelt about a hundred yards up the river near the farmhouse but if he went for it he would lose sight of Algy. He saw him bob up and disappear again. He was quite near the weir now — would he be able to grip hold of the slippery surface and save himself from being swept over it? Charlie hesitated a little longer willing him to surface, then he saw him close to the roaring waters of the weir trying desperately to grab the edge of the weir. He managed to wedge himself against it but was in the middle of the river. Charlie tried to tell him he was going for help, to hang on but the roaring sound of the water falling drowned his voice so he ran as fast as his legs would carry him, never had his club foot seemed so restricting. When he reached the lifebelt he realised even if Algy could grab it he would never have the strength to pull him back on his own.

He ran to the house and picked up the 'phone, after what seemed an eternity the postmistress answered. "Send help to the weir as quick as you can," he gasped and slamming the 'phone down ran back to where Algy was still clinging and wedged. Charlie knew his men would be ploughing at the far side of the farm about half a mile away and there was no one else around.

If he could get the lifebelt to Algy at least it would keep him afloat until help arrived. He threw it but it landed well short, he hauled it in and tried again, this time a little nearer. After about six throws he managed to get it near enough to Algy with the help of the fast-flowing water and he was able to grab it but dare not move in case he was swept away. He was getting very cold and was fervently hoping he would not lose consciousness. Charlie could do little to reassure him as the noise from the rushing water made it impossible to make himself heard.

In a while he heard men's voices and turned to see two young men running towards them. "Thank God you have come," he gasped as they took hold of the rope. They all pulled together and it was not long before they were dragging Algy up the bank where he collapsed. They carried him back to the house and telephoned for the doctor.

Young Dr. Pullen arrived in due course in his bull-nosed Morris by which time Algy had regained consciousness. "He will live," he pronounced, "but keep him good and warm." He listened to Charlie's version of their exploits, then turning to Algy and with mock seriousness he said, "Serves you right for putting the trout back, we could have had him for supper!" Algy spoke for the first time since his ordeal. "Not that one, Doctor," he said, "he is rather special." The doctor suggested a drop of whisky in some hot milk would be the best thing for Algy. "It won't do you any harm," he said, "you have had quite an afternoon. In fact I won't say no to a small one," and the young rescuers didn't say no either, and while they headed for the kitchen he went into the hall and rang Louie.

"He must stay here the night but should be fine by morning," he told her.

"You don't suppose the elderberry wine caused him to fall," said Louie after he had described Algy's narrow escape."

"I should not think so but it may have helped to keep out the cold and contributed to keeping him alive," he said hoping to allay her fears. "Luckily he is a very strong man."

The Knappp family at Clanfield, a village a few miles from Eaton Hastings, owned a foundry which made farm machinery.

Their daughter, Janey, was about Louie's age and the two had become friends. The two families often spent an evening together either at Kilminsters or Clanfield. Louie told Algy she had invited them the next evening and "I have asked Charlie too," she said.

"You scheming hussy," he said.

"Don't tell me you hadn't thought of it?"

"I won't say it hadn't crossed my mind. They would be right for each other in my opinion and that lovely old house needs a woman's touch."

The evening went well and they played cards until midnight.

Louie had not seen Algy so relaxed and happy for a long time. Charlie was his usual friendly self but Louie felt he was deliberately distancing himself from Janey. *Perhaps he is just shy with girls*, she thought.

Mr and Mrs Knapp plainly enjoyed his company and the topic of farming and farm machinery inevitably came into the conversation in spite of Mrs Knapp and Louie's protestations. After a final 'one for the road' the Knapp's chauffeur was at the wheel of their limousine, having spent a pleasant evening in Louie's kitchen in the company of Grace Wheeler and Sally. Louie's little nursemaid who had come to Kilminsters straight from school and was really good with Edwin.

"Its been a good evening," said Algy as they made ready for bed, "but I don't think your little plan is working out very well. I thought Charlie was a bit cool with Janey".

"I think he was a bit shy," said Louie with not much conviction. "I have been thinking. You know you promised me a honeymoon, well do you think we could get away for a few days. Janey is so good with little Edwin and she has always said she would take care of him if we ever wanted to go away, and Sally would help her."

"Do you mean for Janey to stay here?"

"Yes, and I am sure Charlie would keep an eye on the farm for us."

Algy was thoughtful, "Well it is a fairly slack time, but it must only be for a few days."

"I will not be parted from Edwin for more than four days at most," she said.

"Where shall we go?" said Algy.

"Shall we go to Weymouth?" she replied. "They say the bathing is good there and I know how you love a good swim!"

"Any more remarks like that and I will change my mind," he said, pulling her down beside him on the sofa. "I never want to get into cold water again, but I think Weymouth would be nice. You make the arrangements. Check with Janey first, of course."

Janey was thrilled at the prospect of staying at Kilminster, she loved children and felt quite honoured to be entrusted with little Edwin.

Louie booked a room at the Hotel Burden right on the sea front. At last all was arranged, it was the first time they had been away together. As the train steamed out of the station Louie had a moment of panic at the thought of leaving their precious baby, but she knew Algy really needed this holiday and consoled herself with the thought that it was only for a few days.

The carriage started to fill up, two soldiers and two land army girls. Being the third year of the war most young men were in uniform unless they were medically unfit and although Algy was tired his looks didn't pity him. Working in the open air gave him a ruddy complexion. The soldiers piled their kit on to the luggage rack and sat down, they were talking among themselves. Presently, in quite a loud voice one said "Well it's alright for some.

Algy rose to the bait and was about to speak but Louie was quick to intercede. "My husband is a farmer, young man," she said. "Perhaps you have heard it said an army marches on its belly — well someone has to produce the food not just for the army but for everyone."

"I'm sorry ma'm," said the soldier. "I was feeling bad-tempered, my mate and I are on our way back to the front." Louie thought back with sadness to the day of Dick's departure and silently prayed they would be safe.

It was not long before they were all engaged in friendly conversation. The land army girls, it transpired, were billeted not far from Kilminsters and gratefully accepted Louie's invitation to visit them when they returned from their leave and they all promised to write to the soldiers.

The sun was shining when they eventually reached Weymouth, the platform was crowded with sailors with kitbags, waiting for trains. The smell of the sea and the bustle and excitement of the station was all so alien to them. "I have never seen so many sailors," said Louie tucking her arm through Algy's, "lets walk to the hotel it is such a lovely afternoon. Algy picked up their luggage.

"I am getting hungry," he said. "I hope we get a good supper at the hotel."

"It will be dinner," said Louie, "they have dinner in the evening."

"Whatever it is I am ready for it," he replied. "The sea air is giving me an appetite."

"You have always got an appetite," said Louie. When the hotel came in sight Algy looked taken aback, it was very imposing.

"Can we afford it?" he asked.

"It is our very first holiday together, lets make it a good one, after all it is only for a few days."

"We will too,' he said, slipping his free arm round her waist, "there is so much to see and not having to get up for milking at five o'clock in the morning will seem very strange. I hope they will manage alright."

"Of course they will," said Louie, "no one is indispensable." Though she knew the men would have to work very hard without him and she resolved to take them back some gifts and slip a little extra into their pay packets, Algy left the money side of the farming to Louie as well as the book keeping.

The next day after a hearty breakfast, they went for a walk down to the harbour to see the boats but there was so much security they were not allowed to get very near so they went for a stroll round the sadly neglected gardens. The men who were not 'called up' were more gainfully employed, mostly helping with the fishing. They went one day to Lulworth Cove and one day to Osmington Mill and had one of their famous cream teas. The time went so quickly, but they resolved to come again.

They spent the last day shopping for presents to take back. "Have you enjoyed it?" said Algy as they sat in the train heading for home.

Louie nodded. "Every minute," she said, "but right now I can't get home quickly enough to see Edwin."

"Me, too,' he said. Jake was at the station with the trap and it was not long before they were trotting up the drive to Kilminsters.

The first to greet them was Skip, wild with excitement, little stumpy tail wagging madly and there was Janey with Edwin in her arms followed by Grace and Sally. That evening Charlie came round to tell them how everything was on the farm, he stayed until late and Louie was disappointed to see he still seemed distant towards Janey, whom she had persuaded to stay for a few more days. The nights were beginning to draw in and they sat round a log fire and chatted about all that had happened the last few days until Charlie rose reluctantly to take his leave. Algy walked out to his car with him. They stood in the moonlit drive, filling the cool air with the smell of their pipe tobacco.

Algy broke the silence. "What do you think about Janey," he asked.

Charlie gave him a sideways look. "She is very nice," he answered. "We hoped you would have lost your shyness with her by now."

"I am not shy," said Charlie, "but try not to show my feelings for her. I am sure she would not look twice at a cripple like me".

"Don't you believe it. If you ask me she is in love with you. It's as plain as a pikestaff. Louie said to invite you to supper tomorrow and we can have a hand of whist while Janey is here to make up the four."

Charlie thanked him, cranked up his car and headed for Buscot in thoughtful mood. Dare he hope that Algy's prediction could be true. He had become very attracted to Janey but took it for granted that she would not be interested in him. He had never had much time for girls, as he once told Algy, most of his life seemed to be spent sitting on a three legged stool milking cows. *Why, he wondered, did milking stools always have three legs.*

He had the best herd of shorthorns in the neighbourhood and was justly proud of them. He and Algy had a lot in common, the love of cows high on their priorities.

Louie and Janey had combined their cooking skills and in spite of rationing had produced a tasty supper. They played cards for about an hour then gathered round the fire for drinks. After a while Louie said, "I can hear Edwin crying. Come with me Algy, he settles better for you."

After they had gone from the room Charlie looked at Janey. "I did not hear him, did you?" Janey shook her head and they both burst out laughing. Charlie joined Janey on the sofa. "I think we should oblige them, don't you?" he said, slipping his arm round Janey. That was the start of a whirlwind romance and by Christmas they were married.

FIVE

All in all it had been a good year, the farm was showing good profits and they were able to pay off some of the back rent. To everyone's intense joy and relief the war had ended.

James had returned and visited them, staying a while at Harlesford and Kilminsters before travelling to his home in Derbyshire. "The poor lamb looks worn out," Henrietta told Louie on the 'phone, "but he is alive and in one piece, that is the main thing."

During James's stay at Kilminsters, little Edwin, now a year old, was taken very poorly. James said he was sure it was an asthma attack. Dr. Pullen was sent for and he confirmed James's diagnosis. "Is it in the family?" he asked. Algy said his grandfather suffered with it.

"It often misses two generations," said the doctor.

James nodded agreement. "I have heard that," he said.

They had a long discussion exchanging their knowledge and giving Algy and Louie advice on how to cope with little Edwin when he had an attack.

After Dr. Pullen had taken his leave, James expressed his opinion that he deemed them fortunate in having such a caring and knowledgeable doctor. Algy went out to start the milking and for the first time since his return Louie was alone with James. They sat in silence for some time, each with their own thoughts, then James said, "I envy you your happiness, Louie, and I have tried to come to terms with the fact that you are married to someone else. I think I will go home tomorrow before I am tempted to betray Algy's trust in me. It is good of you both to have me and

I have enjoyed my stay."

As Louie looked into his eyes she knew in her heart that she had made a big mistake in marrying Algy, his quick temper and sulky ways had come to the fore lately and Louie remembered his sister Kate trying so diplomatically to warn her. "I don't want to see your heart broken Louie, much as I will love to have you as a sister," she had said.

Dear Kate, I think we should visit them soon. While she was reminiscing Louie felt a shiver down her spine. James noticed her sharp intake of breath and asked if she was alright.

"Someone walking over my grave," she replied. "On reflection, why don't you stay another day or two, you could come with us to visit Algy's family."

"Temptress — you know how I love visiting Wheatfield. Do you think he would mind?"

"Of course he wouldn't," Louie assured him, "and I know they will love to see you. We will go and ask him now." Algy gladly fell in with their suggestion. James picked up a spare milking stool and pail and joined the milkers. "I am a bit out of practice," he said to Algy who was whistling softly and squeezing out the jets of milk in a steady rhythm. "It's like riding a bike, once you have mastered it you never forget," he replied.

Louie went in to 'phone Kate. She had never mastered the art of milking, having suffered an attack of rheumatic fever when she was a girl which had left her eyesight impaired and on previous attempts at milking, the cow would swish its tail and send her spectacles crashing to the floor. "Blow that for a game of soldiers," she had said to herself. " I think I will leave that job to the menfolk."

She was about to pick up the 'phone when it rang, making her jump. She lifted the receiver and was surprised to hear Ida's voice, it was usually Kate who 'phoned from Wheatfield. "Is that you Louie?" Ida's voice sounded strange and distressed. "What is it Ida?"

Louie thought of her father-in-law, Edwin, who was noticeably getting very frail of late. "It is Kate," sobbed Ida, "she has fallen down the stairs and broken her neck. We don't know how it happened she must have tripped."

"We will get there as soon as we can," promised Louie and with a heavy heart went out to impart the sad news to Algy. She knew how devoted he was to his sister as was all the family, in fact she was loved and respected by everyone who knew her. James was a tower of strength and everyone felt comforted by his presence.

Louie knew the admiration she felt for him, the quiet decisive way he handled every eventuality was stirring her emotions and she made sure she was not left alone with him. It was with some relief that when she and Algy returned to Kilminsters James had been persuaded to stay at Wheatfield for a while longer.

The shock had been too much for Edwin, he was very ill and in spite of James's ministrations within a fortnight he followed his daughter to the tiny churchyard in the middle of a field according to his wishes, on a waggon pulled by two of his favourite horses. The church looked for all the world as if it had dropped from heaven straight into the field, there was no road to it, not even a track across the meadow.

The breathtaking view of the surrounding Oxfordshire countryside and the peace and tranquillity of the place made it feel so right for such a peace-loving man as Edwin to finally rest.

SIX

Doreen Louie was born on peace Thanksgiving Sunday, the sixth of July 1919. There were celebrations throughout the land and the young maternity nurse was not best pleased the baby chose that day to put in an appearance. Louie felt quite guilty keeping her from the parties and church services which were held to celebrate the end of that terrible war.

Algy and Sid the cowman had been kept busy on that day with a difficult calving and when at last the heifer calf was born the decision was unanimous, she would be called Doreen after the new baby. Sid followed Algy into the house to see little Doreen and 'wet the baby's head' before starting the afternoon's milking.

Algy bought a pony and trap for Louie, to enable her to go shopping whenever she needed. Polly was an attractive pony bay with a white star and white socks and Louie thought the world of her.

It was the beginning of October and the nights were drawing in. Kilminsters looked its best in the autumn, the virginia creeper covering the front of the house had turned a delightful shade of red and the garden, now well established, abounding with chrysanthemums and michaelmas daisies.

As Algy walked across the fields to bring the cows in for milking, he stood in amazement. The field was covered with mushrooms. He was very fond of them and looked forward to this time of the year, hoping to find some, but had never in his life seen so many. "We will let the housework go hang today," Louie said to Grace, and leaving Sally to mind the children they went out to gather the unexpected crop. After a hurried midday meal

Louie loaded the trap with baskets of mushrooms and with Sally, baby Doreen in her arms and little Edwin sitting beside her they set out at a brisk trot to share their good fortune with as many of their friends as they could before darkness fell.

Sally loved riding in the trap with her mistress and was really good with the children. Edwin now two years old, was quite a handful. In spite of his asthma attacks he was a happy little lad with an infectious smile.

They were heading for Faringdon and making good time when suddenly a big limousine shot out of a side turning so close to Polly's head that the startled pony stopped in her tracks and ran backwards, sending the trap down the bank and uptipping it into a dry ditch. The occupants and contents — mainly mushrooms — went tumbling out. Fortunately, the pony, though trembling with fright, stood still.

There was a screech of brakes and two men ran towards the upturned trap as Louie was getting to her feet. Sally was sitting on the bank still holding the baby in her arms. "Are you alright?"

"Yes, but where is Edwin?"

Louie was distraught, *please god, let him be alright,* as she searched around. Then a faint whimper came from the ditch and there he was under an upsidedown washing basket with mushrooms covering his little body and just his head visible. As Louie picked him up and checked that he was unhurt she heard a familiar voice at her shoulder saying "thank god" and she realised that it was Lord Faringdon and his chauffeur looking anxiously at Edwin who was smiling through his tears happy to be in his mother's arms.

"Louie, what can I say," his Lordship's face revealed the intense relief he was feeling at discovering no one was hurt.

"It's alright, we are all in one piece". Louie had handed Edwin to Sally and was unbuckling the harness, the chauffeur was attempting to help but his hands were shaking so much he was not making a very good job of it.

"He's a bit 'cack-handed," Sally whispered to Louie, "and not much of a driver either". To Louie's embarrassment Lord Faringdon had overheard and whispered back: "He had a real fright you know, he is not used to such a powerful car, being new to the job and no doubt nervous. He will be alright given time."

After they had righted the trap and picked up the mushrooms that were not too badly damaged it was getting rather late, Lord Faringdon suggested that he would take them to Louie's friends. Louie thanked him as she said it was a shame to waste them.

Louie made light of the incident to Algy at teatime not wishing to alarm him unduly and together they laughed at the idea of their mushrooms being delivered by Rolls Royce, but she knew how lucky they were to have escaped injury. That Polly was unhurt, and the trap and harness unscathed, was nothing short of a miracle.

Two years after Doreen was born the stork visited Kilminsters again and what was to have been another boy turned out to be another girl, to Algy's disappointment, so the arranged name of Jack turned into Janet and as Louie's father Tom was ailing they decided to please him this time and call her Janet Latham. Algy was thoughtful, "Latham is not a christian name," he remonstrated, "and it is a rum name for a girl."

"Well we can hardly call her Tom" said Louie, and I think Janet Latham has a good sound and is unusual, so Janet Latham Hutt was decided upon.

Janey always looked forward to her visits to Kilminsters, but they were even more frequent now. She loved children and longed for a baby of her own but so far no luck, so with the Kilminsters brood, three under four years of age, she was a most welcome visitor.

It was evident that Janet was favourite though she loved them all, the new baby was special to her, she had been at Kilministers when she was born and Nurse Bennett, anxious to speak to Dr. Pullen before he departed, entrusted the new baby to Janey as she hurried from the room.

Why, thought Louie, was Dr. Pullen here, it was a very sraightforward birth. What she had not been told was that Doreen, the day before, had been taken very ill.

It was a particularly hot summer in 1921 and though only mid-July the harvesting had started and Sally had carried the tea down to the workers in the cornfields and lent a hand putting the sheaves of corn into stooks while keeping an eye on the children.

By evening, Doreen was very poorly indeed and Nurse Bennett sent for Dr. Pullen who conspired with Algy not to tell Louie the reason for his visit as he did not want to worry her. "I was just passing and thought I would see how you were," he said plausibly. He had diagnosed Doreen as having a very severe attack of sun stroke and said he would call in the morning.

Nurse Bennett and Sally took turns to sit with the little girl through the night, by morning her temperature had subsided slightly and she was sleeping. Grace Wheeler had stayed the night insisting she would be needed to look after Edwin and prophesying correctly, as it happened, that the baby would come the next day.

When the nurse, weary from her disturbed night, went into the kitchen there was a lovely fire in the range, the kettle singing and bacon sizzling in the big iron frying pan.

Grace was on her hands and knees scrubbing the flagstone floor and Edwin sitting astride her back saying "gee-up, wee wee". She had encouraged him to call her 'wee wee' when he could not say Mrs. Wheeler, and now that his vocabulary had considerably improved, 'wee wee' was still 'wee wee' and would always be. Her cheeks were aglow with the exertion of scrubbing and her eyes were reflecting the concern she was feeling as she asked after Doreen. Easing Edwin gently to the floor she stood up, wiping her hands on her sacking apron before making the tea as she listened to Nurse Bennett's account of the little girl's progress. It was lucky you were here nurse. Grace had taken to Nurse Bennett. *Different from the last nurse when Doreen was born she thought.*

Shortly after Janet was born there was a telephone call one morning from Lord Faringdon's butler, inviting Louie and Algy to dine with his Lordship that evening. *No time to buy a new frock,* thought Louie as she searched through her wardrobe wondering what to wear on such an occasion.

Algy had been the proud owner of a car for about two months now. It was bright green with a canvas hood that folded down like that of a pram. It had many brass fitments and the kerosene headlamps were also brass, it shone in all its glory as it swept up the long drive to Lord Faringdon's mansion.

After dinner they sat on the terrace. *I will remember this evening for the rest of my life,* thought Louie as she sipped her glass of sherry and gazed with admiration at the well kept gardens.

"I am sorry about the short notice" said Lord Faringdon, "but I wanted to talk to you rather urgently. You know I am on a lot of committees and consequently hear things before they become public knowledge and it has come to my notice that a very nice farm is coming up for rent. Now please do not think I want to lose you as tenants, but I know Algy is trying to obtain more land and this farm has six hundred acres."

"But we love Kilminsters, Sir," Louie interjected, "I never want to leave it."

"Well go and have a look at Lower Farm and let me know what you think. I am quite sure you will feel as I did, that it is right for you. It is a lovely old house and there are six cottages and Langford is a very nice village."

"We will go tomorrow," said Algy, "and I will let you know straight away."

Little was said on the short journey home, Algy knew how Louie felt about Kilminsters, he loved it too, but the idea of a six hundred acre farm did appeal to him. "We may not like it," he said at last, "but I think we should go and have a look, it is good of him to think of us."

When the car pulled up at the drive gate at Lower Farm they both knew this was to be their home.

The big stone house, in spite of being empty and the garden slightly overgrown, looked inviting, and fond as she was of

Kilminsters Louie fell in love with Lower Farm even before they had looked inside.

As they entered through the church-style porch with bench seats on either side and through the heavy oak door into the large square hall, their voices echoing through the empty house, Algy put his arms round Louie. "What do you think?" but he knew what her answer would be.

"His Lordship is right, of course, but is it out of our bounds — financially?"

"We will walk the farm then go home and do some sums." Algy was fired with enthusiasm. "I would be able to increase the dairy herd and later more sheep, but we must not get our hopes up too much".

Louie loved the house, the oak panelled dining room, the drawing room with white panelling, there was a breakfast room and a real farmhouse kitchen with an outsized kitchen range and beyond the scullery a very large dairy.

After walking round the farm there was no doubt in their minds and they wasted no time in driving straight to Lord Faringdon's residence. "I will do what I can," he assured them, "but of course, it is not entirely up to me. I knew the previous tenant who has just retired and have visited on occasions. It would be nice if I could still visit."

"That it would," said Algy. "I never thought I would want to leave Kilminsters but I think I will be disappointed if we don't get Lower Farm. I wonder how soon we will know."

"There is a meeting of the owners, the Church Commissioners next week. I will put your name forward with my recommendations and let you know what transpires."

The next few days seemed like an eternity and when a 'phone call came from Lord Faringdon's butler saying his Lordship would like a word with them they tidied themselves up and jumped in the car without delay. The old butler ushered them into the morning room where his Lordship was reading the daily papers. "I think the news is good," he said when they were seated. "The

Committee is anxious to meet you and have arranged a meeting the day after tomorrow if that is convenient to you. They would like to see you both if that is possible."

"Of course it is," they spoke in unison.

"I hope to be at the meeting and I see no reason why you would not be accepted as tenants. I wish you well, even though I will miss you at Kilminsters."

The butler interrupted at that moment bringing in coffee, he carefully spread a little lace cloth on the coffee table and proceeded to pour the coffee from a beautiful silver pot into minute bone china coffee cups.

The hard farm work had resulted in Algy's hands being very large indeed and Louie tried not to smile as she watched him crook his little finger and lift the tiny cup to his lips. She prayed that he would not drop it. Without daring to look in Lord Faringdon's direction she instinctively knew he had noticed when he called the butler back as he had almost reached the door and quietly asked him to bring another pot of coffee and three breakfast cups. "I am rather thirsty," he added.

Full marks for diplomacy, thought Louie. Algy, so earnestly talking about their prospects of getting the tenancy of Lower Farm was quite oblivious.

When the day came for the meeting Lord Farington had arranged for Algy and Louie to travel up to London with him in the Rolls Royce.

"I do hope that chauffeur has improved his driving," Sally said to Grace who was giving a final polish to Algy's gaiters. He had decided to dress in his breeches and gaiters even if he might look a bit out of place in London streets.

It was a long drive and Louie was pleased to note that the chauffeur had indeed improved his driving and had become very confident. She had to admire the way he found his directions when they reached London.

As it happened the boots and gaiters played a significant part in the decision of the Committee. They had met and talked at some length with Algy and Louie who were then asked to leave the room.

"Well, I liked them," said one gentleman, who seemed to have a lot of sway, "and did you notice Mr. Hutt's boots? Now I always look at a man's boots — if he has clean shoes or boots you can bet he will keep his farm clean and tidy". There were nods of agreement.

When Lord Faringdon came into the ante-room where Algy and Louie were sitting, his beaming smile told them what they had been waiting to hear. "I wish you luck and happiness at Langford," he said, shaking their hands, "though I must reiterate that I will miss you at Kilminsters."

When they got home and told Sally and Grace what had transpired, Sally at once agreed to go to Langford, but Grace was most unhappy at hearing their news as it would be too far for her to go daily. Louie suggested that she may like to work for the new tenants, but she shook her head. "No, I will retire now," she said, "though I shall miss you all, especially the children."

She hugged Edwin who was sitting on her lap. "We will come and see you often," promised Louie, "and you must visit us."

She knew she would miss Grace very much and she started having reservations about leaving Kilminsters.

Next day Louie felt the need to be alone to think, and took a walk to the heronry. *This is something else I am going to miss,* she thought as she sat down on her favourite log.

A heron flew down and settled on to a nearby tree. She marvelled at such a large bird managing to land so gracefully and grip on to the comparatively small branch which overhung the lake. She watched with fascination as the beady eyes scanned the water, then a sharp dip and a silvery flash on the end of the long beak, then it was gone. *That's your dinner,* thought Louie and decided it was time to get back and make a meal for her own family.

As she was about to make a move she heard a twig snap and turning round, a black boot appeared through a gap in the hedge followed by a rather dishevelled looking man she had never seen before. She was sure he was not local. She knew the gamekeepers on the estate and the likely poachers but they would not be walking the woods at this time of day. He had seen her and was striding towards her. Panic stricken she tried to stand up, her first instinct was to run but she could not move.

As he approached his cheery "Good morning, m'am" helped to allay her fears and she felt more reassured when he was close enough for her to observe his well cut, if rather crumpled, overcoat and in spite of a night's stubble his smiling face and kindly eyes.

"May I?" he indicated her log and before she could reply he had seated himself. "I am sorry to intrude but I saw a heron flying in this direction and was hoping to get a closer look at it. I did not expect to find this," he indicated the herons starting to build their nests in the high branches of nearby trees.

"I hope you mean them no harm," Louie at last found her tongue.

"Far from it," he replied. "I am an ornithologist. Next to my wife and children, birds are my great passion. I know I look like a scarecrow but I have spent the night in a barn near here studying the habits of a pair of barn owls. By the way, the name is Harry, Harry Rook."

He held out his hand, Louie took it rather apprehensively, "Louie Hutt," she returned the introduction.

"Pleased to meet you," he said with a firm handshake. Louie had seen the barn owls and knew the barn where they resided, it was on their farm and that she knew to be authentic but an ornithologist looking like a 'scarecrow' with 'Rook' as his surname could he really be telling the truth? As he chatted enthusiastically so thrilled to have found the heronry and full of admiration for the lovely birds she felt he must be genuine.

"I really must go and get the dinner for my family," she said at last when she could get a word in edgeways, "you would be very welcome to join us. It is only rabbit stew today."

His eyes lit up. "You do really mean that?" he said.

"Then you can meet your landlord," and in answer to his quizzical glance — "well you have been sleeping in my husband's barn. I know about the barn owls but I must confess to not being interested enough to sit up all night with them, but we do love them and are looking forward to the chicks hatching."

They walked back to the farm. Louie was a fast walker but she was having difficulty keeping up with this long striding man. *I expect he is hungry* she thought and hoped there would be enough stew. *I will pop some dumplings in, that will make it go further.*

Harry, it transpired was really a farmer, the bird watching was a hobby. He lived in Devon and had stopped at the village inn while touring the area and in conversation with a local man had learned about the barn owls. He told Louie he was looking round the district to try and find a farm as his wife's parents lived at Lechlade and were not in good health so they needed to be nearer to them. "She has never really settled in Devon," he said. When Algy mentioned that they were moving to a larger farm Harry become very interested and enquired if a tenant had been found for Kilminsters yet. "This is just the sort of place I am looking for," he said.

"We would have to ask Lord Faringdon, our landlord," said Algy, "I will ring him after dinner if you like."

When Algy came back from telephoning his Lordship he was smiling broadly. "'You may be in luck," he told Harry. "He has not found a tenant for Kilminsters yet and has invited us for a cup of tea this afternoon."

"I must smarten up a bit." Harry was on his feet in a flash. "My car and luggage is at the inn."

"You are welcome to stay the night here" said Algy. "Isn't he Louie?"

"Of course, which would you like, Harry, the spare room or the barn?"

"I think I'll plump for the spare room if I may, though I would like to think that I may visit the barn again, hopefully many times."

"We shall keep our fingers crossed for you," rejoined Algy.

"Try and be ready for half past three, his Lordship is a stickler for punctuality and we don't want to make a bad impression. And he said to be sure to bring Louie, he wants you to see his garden, he knows how you love the spring flowers,"

They were ushered into the elegant drawing room by the butler where they were soon joined by his Lordship. Harry was very impressed. The tea table was placed in a bay window which overlooked the garden and was adorned with a lace tablecloth and overflowing with sandwiches, home made cakes and crumpets served piping hot from a silver dish.

In conversation Louie explained about Harry's love of birds and how they had met at the Heronry, omitting the fact that she was scared half to death at his appearance through the hedge. Lord Faringdon was justly proud of his heronry and to hear it praised so eloquently by Harry soon put their acquaintanceship on the right footing.

After tea and much discussion, farming being the main topic, Lord Faringdon turned to Louie, "I've something to show you in the conservatory," he said, "if you gentlemen will excuse us for a few minutes." He took her arm and led her through the hall. As he opened the conservatory door Louie was quite taken aback with the sheer splendour, the exotic plants, many in full bloom.

He was watching her face, her eyes shining with admiration "I knew you would like it but this is not the only motive I had for wanting a quiet word with you. I wanted to ask you for your opinion of Harry Rook." *I wish you had not asked me,* thought Louie, but she answered him directly. "I only met him this morning, so am not in much of a position to judge, but on acquaintance I trusted him or I would not have asked him home, but what he is like as a farmer I really would not know. Would it be a good idea to let your estate manager go and have a look at his farm in Devon before committing yourself — that is, if you like him, of course. Algy seems to be getting on well with him and I think the local bird population would be in safe hands, especially the rooks!"

They laughed. "No more rook pies at Kilminsters! I have heard you are a dab hand at making rook pie. I have never tasted it myself," he added as an afterthought.

"That we can remedy — the next one I make you must come to supper and of course bring your wife, if she would care to, but don't expect my cooking to compare with that of your famous cook — it was a lovely tea, the cakes were delicious."

"I know my wife would love to come but she is not at home very much. Most of her time is spent in Switzerland on account of her health. The children are at boarding school. I miss them all as I shall you and Algy when you go to Lower Farm, Louie."

"Langford is not very far and I hope you will visit us often." They wandered round the conservatory admiring the blooms before returning to the drawing room.

Harry was happy about the suggestion of the estate manager looking at his present farm. "He'll not fault my farming," he said confidently in his very Devonshire accent.

"Then if your references are satisfactory I am sure we shall be in business."

Harry beamed and standing up shook his Lordship's hand vigorously. "As long as it includes allowing me to visit your heronry, sir."

"It has been said that it is good luck to have a rookery on your farm, but I like to think my heronry is my good luck," said Lord Faringdon, "and of course you may visit."

A few days later when Louie took the 'phone to Lord Faringdon he sounded in good spirits. "I have decided to let Harry Rook be custodian to your precious Kilminsters, Louie," he told her. "I have had glowing reports about his farming and his references are first class, and Louie, I think his good firm handshake made up my mind."

Louie smiled, remembering her first handshake from Harry, reassuring at the time. She thought about that first meeting and the subsequent consequences, fate can play some funny tricks.

"I hope his wife will like it," she said.

"Harry is sure she will and is going to bring her to see the farm as soon as they can arrange it, at your convenience, of course."

"We shall look forward to meeting her," Louie was trying to conjure up an image of Harry's wife and felt instinctively that she would like her.

SEVEN

Came the day of the big move, Michaelmas Day, the twenty ninth of September, it was the most usual day for farms to change hands. Harry had sold his farm, lock, stock and barrel as the distance was too great to drive his stock along the roads, but Algy and his men drove his flock of sheep to Langford and the herd of cows and the pigs were loaded in waggons with nets over them and transported to their new home. Charlie sent a couple of his men to help and Janey came over to help with the children and drive the men back from Langford in Charlie's model T Ford.

Some of the farm workers were staying at Kilminsters to work for Harry and three were going to Langford, which would mean that three of the Lower Farm workers would be sacked, which led to much bad feeling.

They were airing their views at the blacksmith's forge one day. After listening to the sacked men's grievances, the blacksmith suggested giving the new master of Lower Farm the 'rough music'. "We'll show he," said one man who had spent his dinner hour in the public house and was spoiling for a fight, "we'll give he the rough music alright".

It had been a long arduous day but they were finally installed in their new home. Louie and Sally were upstairs getting the children to bed and Algy was still in the cowshed bedding down the cows when it started. About ten men with lanterns came up the drive making the most unholy din, clanging saucepan lids together and banging iron bars on old wash trays, anything that would make a noise.

Telling Sally to stay and look after the children Louie flew down the stairs reaching the hall as they banged on the front door. She opened it and stood in the doorway facing the angry crowd. "Tell he to come out, not hide behind a woman's skirts," said the ring leader.

"If you mean my husband, he is attending to his stock and will not know about this absurd behaviour." Louie's legs were like jelly but she was determined not to let them see how frightened she was.

"Our fight is not with you ma'am, it's with the master".

"Then it is with me and you had better tell me what it is all about."

"It's about the sackings." Louie had guessed that was at the bottom of all this.

"Well," she said, "why do you have to behave in this way?" If you come and see my husband in an orderly fashion I am sure he will do his best for whoever it concerns. He is a fair employer. I grant you he has a temper, that I'll not deny, but he looks after his men and his animals. We will get something sorted out, but if my husband comes in and sees you like this I won't answer for his actions".

The men looked at each other then touched their caps, "Thank you m'am, goodnight," and sloped off into the night.

Louie shut the big oak front door and leaning her back against it took a deep breath, *this is a good start,* she said to herself and resolved not to tell Algy. When she had composed herself sufficiently she ran back upstairs to Sally and the children. Sally looked anxiously at her mistress. Louie explained to her about the sackings and told her of her decision not to tell the master about the rough music, "not tonight at any rate," she said, "he will be exhausted when he gets in and there is no need for him to know." Sally agreed. They tucked the sleeping children in their beds and went downstairs to prepare the supper.

There were two men at the back door in the morning. Louie asked them into the kitchen where she was unpacking china. "I have not told my husband about the carry-on last night," she said to them just before Algy came in.

"These are the men who have been sacked, Algy. I think they are hoping you could perhaps find employment for them."

"This be Carter Burson," the slim dark haired young man introduced his companion, "and I be Walter Hunt," he added.

"Were there not three who received their notice?" asked Louie.

"Stevie would not come, he has worked on this farm man and boy and his wife Zipora has worked in the house — she is a good washer woman and they have got four children," Carter Burson spoke for the first time.

After talking to the men at great length Algy and Louie excused themselves and went into the breakfast room to talk the matter over.

"Couldn't we keep them on," urged Louie, "there will be a lot to do to pull the farm round." So the two men were re-engaged. "Tell Stevie and his wife to come and see me," said Algy "my missus will be needing help in the house and if Stevie is as good a worker as you say I dare say we will find employment for him."

Later that morning when Louie answered the knock at the back door, there they stood, Stevie and Zipora, the most dilapidated old pram Louie had ever seen, and four of the bonniest children — all the image of their mother — smiling up at her. Zipora was just as plump as her husband was thin. Louie took to her on sight and felt relieved to think she had so quickly found someone to take the place of Grace. Algy soon made up his mind that he would like to have Stevie on his payroll.

"Well, Stephen my lad, can you be in the cowshed at six o'clock sharp for milking?"

"That I can sir, but folk round here call I Stevie. I 'ent never been called Stephen."

"Right then, Stevie, see you in the morning."

"And do I call you Zipora or Zippie," Louie asked Stevie's wife. "Anything you like as long as I have got the job, ma'am."

"Start as soon as you like, there is plenty to do, and I will càll you Zipora, I think it is a nice name."

Louie pretended not to notice the tears running down her face as she turned away to pull the covers across the baby. "I will be down in the morning," she said over her shoulder as she followed her husband through the door.

"Don't forget to bring your milk can," Louie reminded them "and you had better take this for tonight," she handed them a large enamel jug of milk. All the farm workers received a can of milk night and morning, the tin cans with lids and handles were left at the back door to be filled from the pails of milk from the 'house cow'.

Louie stood at the window and watched Stevie and his family trundling home and felt sure she had done the right thing in not letting Algy know about the 'rough music', he would never have taken any of them on, she was sure of that, and the thought of Stevie being out of work and the subsequent possible suffering to that charming family she did not wish to contemplate.

Carter Burson was married with a young son Billy. His wife was a good looking woman with an abundance of beautiful red hair twisted into a bun at the back of her head. Louie decided when she met her that she was not a happy woman. She had an aloof air about her which made communication difficult and it was evident that whatever was troubling her she would never divulge.

The other man now reinstated was, they decided, not much more than a lad. His name was Adam and on first acquaintance he appeared to be 'two pennies short of the proverbial shilling'. The impediment in his speech did not help to allay the fact, but after patiently talking for a while, Algy found him to be very intelligent, especially where horses were concerned, and he consigned him to help Carter Burson in the stables, to the lad's immense satisfaction. He had only done odd jobbing round the house previously and to him it was an important promotion, especially when Algy told him he would be taught to plough, to be in charge of a team of horses and to be able to plough a straight furrow was beyond his wildest dreams. He was on cloud nine when he hastened home that evening to tell his parents, but he was brought down to earth with a bump however when he went to work the next morning and was assigned a wheelbarrow and shovel and confronted with ten very large horses. Carter Burson was piling food into their mangers.

The mucking out proved to be a never-ending job, as soon as he thought he had nearly finished, another heap appeared. But he was undaunted, to be with horses was his dearest wish, and though his back was aching with pushing the piled up wheelbarrow to the muck heap he was eager to learn all the skills of caring for the beautiful animals.

All the other men were addressed by their christian names, but no one knew or asked the carter's name, he was always Carter Burson.

Algy soon found that he had inherited a treasure in the carter and when giving the men their orders for the day's work he found himself asking the carter's advice about matters concerning the land such as mowing the grass for haymaking, or sowing the seeds, he would sometimes disagree but the carter usually got his way which Algy had to admit nine times out of ten turned out to be the right one.

Walter Hunt was a good milker, he was an earnest young man dedicated to his work. Algy liked his quiet way with the cows and felt he would fit in well at Lower Farm.

On Fridays, come rain or shine, Louie would go the six miles to Faringdon in the pony trap to get the money from the bank for the men's wages and do some shopping. Sally and the children accompanied her when the weather permitted.

Louie noticed that after every journey Edwin had an attack of asthma. She told Dr. Pullen of this, explaining that she was most particular to wrap him in warm clothing. "Now that is the smell of the horse," he answered decisively, "the little lad is affected by the smell of some animals, the horse is evidently one he must avoid."

Knowing how Sally looked forward to her outings in the trap,

Louie delayed telling her and spent a sleepless night resolving the situation. It was evident that Edwin must not go again. Her mind was made up. She surprised Algy at breakfast time the next morning by telling him she intended to buy herself a car.

Tom had died two years previously and the estate had been settled, mater inheriting most of the money, but a proportion was divided among the children.

Louie was rather apprehensive about driving a car but decided if Janey could do it she jolly well would. "But your car is too big for me," she said, and Algy agreed that it made sense for her to have her own smaller car and they planned an outing to Oxford the following day.

Sally was delighted, though she loved Polly the pony and riding in the trap, to ride in a car was just as appealing, if not more so. The car was delivered to Lower Farm a week later, Louie's heart missed a beat when she saw it standing on the gravel drive in all its glory. She had settled on a Citroen, it was navy blue and had a canvas hood which folded back. She felt it was essential for Edwin to get all the fresh air he could. As she stood listening to the car salesman talking enthusiastically about the merits of her purchase, the way it handled and the extra refinements etc etc, her mind was elsewhere. She felt a little pang of guilt spending so much, she knew how desperately Algy needed to enlarge his sheep flock and decided there and then to let him have some of her inheritance.

Her father had always advised her to keep her own money, but ignoring his advice, after giving the young man tea and taking him to the station in the pony trap, she went in search of Algy to tell him of her decision.

It was coincidental that a fortnight later there was to be the annual sheep sale at Craven Arms in Shropshire. Algy had always wanted to go but now with Louie's money 'burning a hole in his pocket', as the saying goes, he resolved to make the trip. He telephoned his pals Charlie Norman and Harry Rook who took little persuading to join him on his trip.

Louie was not altogether pleased at the thought of being left to run the farm, be it only for a few days, the rambling old house could be a little awe inspiring at night. "You will be alright," Algy assured her. "I will show you how to shoot and you can keep my gun by your bedside."

"Oh no," said Louie, "no way." But Algy was insistent and she finally relented, and hoping against hope not to have to use it, she tucked it under her bed telling him that she was quite capable of handling a gun.

The days leading up to Algy's trip to Shropshire were filled with preparations, Louie packing plenty of very stiffly starched white collars into his suitcase together with a nightshirt and a pair of silver backed hair brushes. Zipora was in the scullery, his brown leather gaiters hanging over one chubby arm and brushing with the other until you could almost see your face in them.

At last, goodbyes were said and Louie watched the car disappear from view with a sense of apprehension. Algy was to pick up his two friends from Buscot and Little Faringdon then drive to Craven Arms. They had discussed going by train but felt it would be more convenient to have the car, so with spare cans of petrol fastened to the running board and an extra spare wheel in case of a puncture, he set off on his journey.

The children had come down from the nursery to say goodbye to their father, Sally was rocking Janet in the pram with one hand and holding on to Doreen with the other. Louie looked round to see Edwin shivering in the cool morning breeze and taking his hand she hurried them all indoors.

She went into the kitchen where Zipora had started her morning's work, the chairs were put on the long oval table and she was on her hands and knees scrubbing the flag stone floor. She took Edwin across to the kitchen range which had already been blackleaded, the hearth whitened and the fender shining like a new pin, rubbing the little lad's hands as she went. Zipora is over working she thought as she surveyed the kitchen, so bright and clean. "I am going to employ a kitchen maid," she said, "you are doing far too much."

Zipora gave a final wipe to the last bit of floor and sitting back on her haunches wiped the perspiration from her forehead with the sleeve of her frock. "My sister's oldest leaves school next week," she said, "and I know she would like to come here to work. So it was settled that she should come and see Louie as soon as she left school.

"I have a long distance call for you," the postmistress announced with great importance when Louie took the telephone that evening. She knew she would be 'having a little listen' but Algy's voice was hardly discernible, the line was so crackly, "Hello Mrs". From the day they were married Algy always called her Mrs, "are you alright?"

"Yes, fine," she answered him and was relieved to hear that they had arrived safely.

When she climbed into bed that night it was many hours before she could get to sleep, the slightest sound seemed to magnify itself, even the owls hooting which normally she would have enjoyed hearing now sounded eerie and unreal. *I will be glad when Algy is back,* she thought. She finally fell into a deep sleep but was soon awakened by the cockerel crowing and she knew it was time to get up and give the men their orders for their day's work. Algy had left instructions but she knew Carter Burson would have the final say regarding his day's work.

As she passed Edwin's bedroom door she could hear the little lad wheezing and coughing and knew he was having an asthma attack. She went into his room to comfort him, the only remedy was 'Potters Asthma Cure' which was burnt in a metal bowl and gave off a strong aromatic smell. She lit the substance and bent over the bed to give him a hug promising to be right back and resolving to get the doctor as soon as possible. She ran down the back stairs and through the kitchen to the back door drawing back the heavy iron bolts she opened it to confront ten men looking at her expectantly waiting in the early morning light,

"Good morning, ma'am," almost in unison. They are a good

bunch she thought as she proceeded to give them their instructions for their day's work until she was confronted with the stocky countenance of Carter Burson. He, like most farm workers, always tied string round their trouser legs, just below the knee. Louie puzzled about this and once asked Algy why they did this. "To stop rats running up," he had replied but she never knew whether to believe him, but supposed it was as good a reason as any.

The Carter touched his cap respectfully and proceeded to tell Louie what he thought he should do that day. She read Algy's instructions and smiled at his final sentence, 'unless he has other ideas' with lots of exclamation marks.

As he strode off she closed the door and ran back to Edwin's bedroom to find Sally had preceded her and was persuading him to drink a cup of tea. 'Poor little mite,' she murmured and Louie could see the concern in her eyes and wondered how soon she dared ring the doctor but knowing in her heart there was little he could do to alleviate Edwin's suffering.

The good doctor made Lower Farm his first port of call, he was so gentle and kind that his very presence made Louie feel easier in her mind. "You are doing everything right," he assured her noting the fire which Zipora had lit in the bedroom grate. "Keep him warm and ring me this evening."

To everyone's relief Edwin's breathing had very much improved by the evening so when Algy telephoned, Louie decided not to tell him of Edwin's quite frightening attack, he had enough to worry about getting the sheep home she thought.

He told her he was pleased with his purchases and Charlie and Harry had also bought some sheep, they would be putting them on the train tomorrow and would she have some men standing by to drive them from the station as soon as the station master lets her know when they arrive. It had been quite a day and when at last she was satisfied that Edwin was sleeping soundly, Louie said goodnight to Sally, who was already in bed and made her way to her bedroom, almost as soon as she had climbed into bed she fell into a deep sleep.

She opened her eyes, someone was shaking her by the shoulder, an urgent firm shake. It took her a few seconds to waken then as she was about to sit up a low "shh" and she realised it was Sally. "What is the matter, is it Edwin?"

"No m'am, there is someone downstairs."

The moonlight shining through the window enabled Louie to see the terror in her eyes. "Are you sure?"

"Oh yes, ma'am, he knocked something over in the dairy and I heard him swear." Louie was out of bed.

"I'll give him swear," she said and dived under the bed to retrieve the gun. She put her arm round the frightened girl, "Don't worry, I expect it is just a tramp."

"As long as it is not him."

"Not who?" Louie spoke aloud then checking herself whispered, "Who are you talking about?"

"Zipora heard in the village that a convict had escaped from Oxford gaol, a dangerous criminal they said, but we did not want to worry you with the master away, and anyway we did not think he would come this way or so far."

"It probably is not him" she said trying to allay Sally's fear. She tried to suppress a shudder as she padded along the passage gripping the gun with one hand and the other arm round Sally.

She went into the bathroom, knowing she would be able to see the dairy from the bathroom window and get a good view of the back door, slowly she pushed up the sash window and peered out on to the moonlit courtyard. She could see the dairy and saw to her dismay that Sally was right, there was someone in the dairy. She saw a shadow move across the window.

She thought of Doreen and Janet in the nursery which was directly above the dairy and was easily accessible up the back stairs. She knew Sally would not have the courage to go to them and she would not dream of asking her to, so hastily she screwed up all her courage and lifting up the gun she pushed the barrel through the open window, she put the butt against her shoulder as her brothers had taught her and with her finger on the trigger she attempted a masculine voice. At first, no sound came, then she heard herself say, "Come out of there you bugger, I have got a gun. If you don't believe me, I'll prove it to you." Her finger closed on the trigger and the kick of the gun against her shoulder nearly knocked her backwards.

Sally gasped, then they both peered and waited. "I have never heard you swear ma'am," Sally whispered.

"Drastic situations call for drastic measures," she answered "but don't let the master know, it is one of his pet hates to hear a woman swear, my father was the same".

"Here he comes!"

The back door opened slowly and a shadowy figure emerged, the agility and speed with which he disappeared into the night convinced Louie this was no tramp, besides most of the 'gentlemen of the road' in the district would know there was no need to steal food from Lower Farm, they never went from there empty handed. So she decided to 'phone the police, though she hated disturbing both the postmistress, who would have to answer the telephone, and the constable in the middle of the night.

This done she went to the kitchen and raked the embers of the range, she pulled out the damper and coaxed the fire to burn up, pushing the kettle over. Sally was checking that the children had not awakened from the gunshot.

By the time the constable arrived Louie and Sally were enjoying a steaming cup of tea. "I have been on the 'phone to the Oxford constabulary and they are sending someone out at once," the young constable announced with great importance, "It will take about an hour to get here from Oxford."

"Shall we go into the dairy and see what he has been up to," said Louie when they had finished their tea.

"I don't see the harm," said the constable, so they trooped through the scullery into the dairy. The floor was awash with milk, the intruder had knocked over a pail of skimmed milk which had been standing on the floor ready for the pigs in the morning. "That is what you heard, Sally," said Louie, "it must have made quite a clatter, no wonder he swore."

The dairy doubled as a pantry. There was a meat safe at one end and along one wall were two lead-lined vats in which the bacon was cured and the hams pickled.

The flitches of bacon lay in the long vat and every day were religiously rubbed with salt and the hams were put in the short vat and were basted with a very special pickle; sugar, salt and juniper berries, being some of the ingredients—the recipes were often handed down from generation to generation. After an allotted time the bacon and hams were wrapped in muslin and hung from beams in the kitchen.

Round the other two walls were wide marble shelves on which pans of milk were placed overnight for the cream to rise and this was skimmed the next day with a metal skimmer and the cream put in a bowl ready for making the butter, the skimmed milk then fed to the pigs.

The constable was scrutinising the milk pan which had been disturbed, with the light of the candle. He spotted a red hair lying on top of the cream. "Don't anyone touch that milk pan. I think I have found the evidence that it is our man. He is reputed to have red hair and a long beard, that is the description we were given."

"What did he do?" asked Louie.

"I don't know, ma'am, but we were told not to tackle him on our own. You had a narrow escape, I would say."

"You mean, he did," said Louie. "I could have shot him and had my husband been at home he probably would have."

The constable smiled and nodded, he had not been in the village long but he had heard of Algy's reputation as being an excellent shot as well as having a very quick temper.

At that moment the front door bell rang. Sally ran to open it and admitted two police sergeants who followed her to the dairy. After introductions the constable lost no time in showing them his discovery, the hair in the milk pan. "Well done," said the most senior of the sergeants. "That is him alright, may I use your 'phone Mrs. Hutt? I must call for reinforcements, but first let us look round to see what else he has taken, besides drinking your milk".

Louie headed for the meat safe. "Pigs trotters!" she exclaimed, "he has stolen Algy's pigs trotters, he is very partial to them and I cooked them ready for his return and the remainder of a joint of boiled beef, oh, and about two pounds of uncooked sausages."

The young constable was finding it difficult not to burst out laughing, the idea of someone actually stealing pigs trotters, to him, was beyond belief. *Boney things,* he thought, *he must have been hungry.* Sally had discovered that a loaf of bread was also missing.

"Enough to keep him going for sometime," said the senior sergeant. "My guess is he will hide in a barn or shed for a while until the hue and cry dies down, but now we know he is in this area I think we will soon find him. First we must search your buildings before your men come to work, though I don't think any harm will come to them. I think he will remain hidden but we will not take any chances."

The dawn was breaking by the time the reinforcements arrived and the milkers who were the first to get to work were surprised to see uniformed police officers bobbing in and out of the buildings. The village constable explained the situation to Stephen Hedges and told him to keep his eyes skinned but if he saw the convict not to approach him. Stephen passed on the information to the other men as they collected their milking stools and pails.

Above the rhythmic sound of the milk squirting into the metal pails there was much talk that morning, the men were usually sleepy at that time and not much conversation ensued but this day was different.

"I wonder where the bugger is," said Walter Hunt. "Could be in the next village by now," said Stephen. "I'll 'ud like to know what he did, they says as how he be a dangerous character."

"That there constable said as the missus shot the master's gun at 'un," rejoined Walter, "pity she missed, I should think."

There was much laughter, then the thought of the missus shooting a gun caused some amusement. After some minutes of silence, Walter remarked, "Well I suppose it is really not a joking matter. It must have been a very frightening experience for the missus and little Sally." There was general agreement and silence reigned as the men got on with the job of filling their pails.

The happenings of the night completely excluded all thoughts of the sheep coming on the train that day. When the telephone rang and the station master told her excitedly that a train was at the station loaded with sheep for Mr. Hutt, her heart missed a beat. She knew the shepherd was at the other end of the farm a mile away and the other men were working in different parts of the farm. She thought of her car, Algy had told her not to attempt to drive it unless he was with her, and she was not sure of what to do. It would take some time to harness the pony and cart, so she grabbed her old bike and pedalled off. By the time she had reached the shepherd she had hailed two more men and sent them hurrying to the station. The sheep leapt and danced out of the railway waggons so pleased to be released from their confined space and into the open air.

The old shepherd stood in admiration saying quietly, "Steady, my beauties." Louie could see he was pleased with Algy's purchases, she wondered how long it would take him to get home from Craven Arms and decided to ring Janey when she got home. She studied the shepherd's weather-beaten face, so full of concern and could not help thinking how lucky they were to have such a dedicated man in their employ. She thought how tired he looked and knew he would have worked hard to prepare for these additional charges.

When the sheep had been driven to their new pastures Louie returned to the farm. After visiting the nursery to check on Sally and the children, she filled a basket with home cured bacon and eggs and other goodies and took it over to the shepherd's cottage, to be greeted by his wife, most anxious to hear first hand the happenings at the farm.

"Is it true you shot a man, ma'am?" Louie laughed.

"Not quite," she said, and thought news travels fast and sometimes gets distorted on the way.

She told the old lady what had happened and did her best to dispel any fears that the criminal was still in the district, but suggested it would be a good idea to keep her cottage door locked until they knew he had been recaptured. She returned to the farm just as Algy arrived. To say she was pleased to see him would be an understatement. There was so much to talk about! When Louie remarked to her husband that he looked tired, he admitted to being 'out on his feet'. Apart from the journey and coping with the sheep, they had stayed in a hotel in Ludlow, which was very near to the cathedral and the clock struck every quarter of an hour, and neither him nor his companions could sleep a wink. "It was so loud Louie, you would not believe it," though he had to admit it did not compare with the drama of Louie's sleepless night.

They both decided their intruder would be far away by now and decided on an early night, sleeping soundly and awakening early, Algy anxious to inspect his new flock of sheep and Louie remembering some chicks were due to hatch.

As soon as breakfast was over they went their separate ways, Algy to the fields and Louie set off to the yard. There was a brick built out-house which she had had converted to house her broody hens. All around the walls were brick built nesting boxes, there was only a very small window high on the wall which made it ideal for the setty hens as they liked it fairly dark and there was a stout wooden door with a catch and bolt on the outside. Twice a day Louie would lift them off their nests for food and water, often getting her hands pecked for her trouble.

I must have forgotten to push the bolt, she thought, as she lifted the latch and entered, heading for the nearest hen, but as she looked down in the dim light her fears were realised. There on the ground lay a little scattering of bones, barely discernible among the hen droppings, but she at once recognised the round shape of pigs trotter bones.

In a state of sheer terror she instinctively knew the convict was behind the door and if she turned and ran he could block her exit, her only chance was to pretend not to know he was there, so with trembling hands and her heart banging so hard she felt sure he would hear it, she lifted off hen after reluctant hen, speaking to them quietly. "There you are then old biddies, eat your breakfast," she said finally and turned to leave. She could see the toe of a boot slightly protruding under the door. "Please God, let me get out," she silently prayed, as she forced her unwilling legs to walk to the open door. She pulled it to behind her and slid the heavy bolt into place.

Walter was crossing the yard carrying full pails of milk which he placed on the ground when he saw Louie running towards him. "It's the convict," she gasped. "He is in the broody hen house, keep guard and don't let anyone undo the bolt, I must go and 'phone for the police."

By the time Algy returned from the fields the village constable had arrived and was talking to Walter and the other milkers who had gathered round. "Whatever is going on?" he said.

The constable explained that the convict was incarcerated in Louie's broody hen house. "I have sent for the sergeant," he said. "I dare not risk losing him, even with the help of your men. I had better wait for the sergeant to arrive."

It seemed an eternity, though it was well under an hour when the police car swept into the drive, braking sharply. Three uniformed policemen jumped out, led by the senior sergeant. Algy greeted them and took them out to the yard where the group of men were standing expectantly with the constable.

After a short consultation, the sergeant walked towards the door of the hen house. "Now lad," he said in a fatherly voice, "it's best for you if you come quietly. Just lie on the floor and put your hands above your head."

"I will come quietly," came the reply, "but don't make me lie in this hen muck. I promise I will come quietly."

There were giggles from the onlookers. "Alright, put your

hands up then." He opened the door to reveal a very dishevelled looking individual sporting a long red beard and in dire need of a wash. He was very soon also sporting a pair of hand cuffs and was being led by two of the policemen towards the car. "I think my wife has prepared some refreshments for you," said Algy and was soon taken up on the offer.

Louie had joined them then and suggested they take the prisoner in through the back door. "He will know the way," she said, which made the unfortunate man smile in spite of himself. "He can wash his hands and face in the scullery." Well fortified they reluctantly took their leave and Algy and Louie walked with them to the car.

As the prisoner was led past Louie he looked round at her, she felt her heart miss a beat expecting him to curse her for being instrumental in his recapture, but after a moment's hesitation, he said, "Thank you ma'am," and added, "by the way, some chicks have hatched under the speckled hen in the corner nest box, looks like a good clutch to me."

"I will go and see to them," she said and after the car had driven off she made for the yard. He can't be all that bad she thought, wondering what he had done to be described as a dangerous criminal.

The sergeant had told Algy confidentially however, that he was awaiting trial for murder and was full of praise for Louie's bravery in capturing him.

When the men went home for their dinner the excitement of the morning was soon public knowledge and by the evening the way Mrs. Hutt had captured the wanted man in her broody hen house was the main topic of conversation, with the workers very much in the limelight and relating the story many times with the assistance of a few mugs of ale in the local inn, the episode was greatly elaborated upon.

The following day Sally went with Louie to help her transfer the hen and chicks into a coop and put them in the orchard. Doreen and Janet were with them but Edwin was riding his tricycle in the drive. He loved his trike and used to let Doreen stand on the back and give her rides round the garden. Between his asthma attacks he was a very lively four year old.

With much clucking and pecking, the mother hen sitting comfortably under Louie's arm, Sally popped the chicks in a basket and soon they were in a coop in the orchard, the chicks tucked under the mother hen.

Louie headed for the kitchen to start the dinner while Sally went in search of Edwin, but he was nowhere to be found. She searched everywhere and finally went in to tell Louie. "I would not have thought he would venture on the road," she said, "but we had better look."

She sat the two girls in the commodious pram and telling Sally to get her bike and go in the opposite direction towards the railway station, she headed at a run for the village asking the few people she could see in the almost deserted street if they had seen Edwin, but without success. It was evident he had not come this way. She reached the farm to see Sally returning from the other direction. "No sign," said Sally, "and I have been a good two miles."

They stood in the drive wondering what to do next when they heard the telephone ringing. Louie ran to answer it, out of breath and almost sobbing with worry she picked up the receiver. "Is that you, Louie," came the familiar voice of Bert Knap.

"Bert, we have lost Edwin," she cried.

"That is why I am ringing," said Bert, "he has just arrived on his trike. He says he has come to dinner and wants to tell Lindsay about a man who was locked in a chicken house."

Lindsay was Mr & Mrs Bert Knap's youngest and only son. There were two girls and then the longed for son who was eight years old now, and Edwin was very fond of him. Lindsay, though twice his age, was very patient with the little lad and enjoyed playing with him. The Bert Knaps lived in a beautiful house in the middle of Clanfield on the opposite side of the road to the Foundry and the Tom Knaps.

It was arranged that Bert and his wife would bring Edwin home after tea and have supper at Lower Farm and hear the saga of the escaped convict.

Sally was crying with relief at hearing Edwin was safe and Louie made them a good strong cup of tea to steady their nerves, while marvelling at how he could have pedalled that tricycle for miles and managed to find the house. It was quite a feat. In spite of everything Louie had to feel rather proud of her brave little son.

The farm was prospering and now, as well as Betty, the kitchen maid, Zipora's oldest daughter, Cissy, was employed as the parlour maid. In the morning she was sweeping and dusting the rooms and in the afternoon she donned a black dress and a white lace trimmed apron, a lace band round her head with black velvet ribbon threaded through and tied at the back. Her duties then were to answer the door to visitors and serve afternoon tea.

She had grown into a very attractive girl, had inherited Zipora's clear skin and abundance of wavy hair and Stephen's long slim legs. Louie had noticed Algy's eyes following her graceful movements as she went about her work but dismissed any suspicious thoughts, realising any man could not help looking at such a pretty young girl.

It was not until she had started off one day in the car to go to Faringdon and discovered that she had left her handbag behind, instead of turning the car in the narrow road she decided it would be just as quick to run back. As she entered the kitchen she found them in a passionate embrace.

Louie was devastated. Too shocked to speak, she walked through the kitchen without a word, picked up her handbag from the hall table and went out of the front door and back to the car. She sat there just staring in front of her, and did not see or hear the bicycle passing her from behind. As he swung his bike round in the road she recognised the station master and as he approached he shouted, "Are you alright, Mrs. Hutt?"

"Yes, thank you, station master," she heard herself say. Then as he cycled on his way she laughed hysterically. "How can I say I am alright. I don't think I will ever be alright again." Then she thought of the children and the effect it would have on Zipora and Stephen if Cissy were to lose her job, after all she is really not much more than a child and in her heart she knew it was Algy's fault. His temper and sulks I can cope with but this is different.

She finally resolved to drive to Buscot and though not wishing to burden her, she thought she would tell Janey, a trouble shared is a trouble halved, Henrietta used to say, and she knew Janey could be trusted.

She started the car and headed to Buscot where she found her friend weeding in the garden. One look told Janey there was something amiss. "I am so glad to see you," she said, "I was longing for a cup of tea and it did not seem worth making one just for me." She slipped her hand through Louie's arm and they went indoors. It was not long before Louie was pouring her heart out to her friend.

"I just don't know what to do," she said.

"And I don't know how to advise you," said Janey. "I have not had any experience in such matters. I just cannot imagine Charlie behaving that way, perhaps I am being too complacent but I have never even given it a thought."

They were silent for a few minutes just sipping their tea, then Louie said, "I don't see how I can leave him. I could not support three children and I certainly could not leave them." The back door opened, they knew it would be Charlie. "Don't tell him," Louie whispered as his footsteps approached the sitting room. Janey wondered how she would explain Louie's tear-stained face. She knew he would be sure to notice. She took the teapot out to the kitchen to make a fresh pot.

Charlie was never one to beat about the bush. "What is the trouble, Louie?" Louie was silent for a moment then she said "Can I trust you not to let Algy know I have told you?"

He nodded. "You can, Louie," he answered her.

By the time Janey returned, Louie had told him briefly the

day's happenings. "I have told Charlie," she said.

"I am so relieved. I did not think I could keep a secret from him or tell him a lie," said Janey. "What advice can we give her? I am at a loss."

Charlie looked serious. "Don't do anything hasty," he said at last. "It is the rook shoot tomorrow, we will see you then."

"I had forgotten all about it, I was on my way to Faringdon to get some things for the lunch".

"I will come over early and give you a hand," said Janey. "I can get what you need on the way."

Driving home Louie's thoughts went back to the years before they were married, the parties at Copcourt, the home of her dear friend, Kate Darvill, and at Manor Farm, a beautiful rambling farmhouse in the middle of Oakley, as well as Algy's home at Wheatfield and her own at Draycot and Harlesford. There were plenty of pretty girls but he only had eyes for her.

When she reached the farm she was soon busy helping Sally with the children and preparing for the shooting party. She went into the scullery and found Cissy sobbing. "Come on, Cissy," she said rather sharply, "we haven't time for that."

"But what will I tell Mam and Dad about having the sack?"

"I have not said anything about dismissing you."

"The master said I must leave," said the distraught girl.

"Well I am mistress of this house and I say you stay. I shall not mention anything to your parents as I don't think it was your fault."

"I only did as I was told," sobbed Cissy. "My Mam said I was to be a good girl, work hard and do as I was told."

There is no answer to that, thought Louie. "Alright then, dry your eyes and come and help me with laying the table. It will save time in the morning," she said as she spread the white damask table cloth over the long dining table. She felt little enthusiasm for the party and fervently wished it had not been arranged.

She had not seen Algy since returning from Buscot, so when she heard him crossing the hall to the breakfast room she decided to follow him, dreading the confrontation which was inevitable. He was standing with his back to her with his gun in his hand which he was about to return to the cupboard. He had been cleaning it ready for the next day's shoot. He turned to face her, they stood in silence for a few minutes, neither knowing what to say.

Algy was the first to speak. "It was not my fault Mrs., the girl led me on. I have given her the sack."

"Please, Algy, don't insult my intelligence. I know to my sorrow whose fault it was and Cissy will be staying in my employ. I will not interfere with the running of the farm or dismiss your workers and I will thank you to leave the running of the house to me."

Louie ran from the room slamming the door behind her. I must not let Cissy see me crying she thought, as she forced back the tears of hurt and anger. Sally had joined Cissy and was helping with the table. "May I arrange the flowers ma'am," she said as Louie joined them.

"You may," she said, pleased to relinquish the task, knowing Sally was particularly adept.

Janey arrived early next morning driving the bull-nosed Morris bringing Louie's shopping. "Harry is picking Charlie up later," she said. They were soon busy in the kitchen. When they were alone, Janey asked Louie what was happening regarding Algy's infidelity. Louie told her that he had excused himself by blaming Cissy. "I really think that hurt the most," she said.

"But it was a good idea to take it out on that cream," said Janey. "I have never seen cream whipped at such a speed."

Louie laughed as she lifted the whisk from the large bowl of cream and piled it liberally on to the dishes of sherry trifle.

"Now I am going to tell you the latest news Charlie heard at market yesterday. Algy did not go so you won't have heard." Louie popped the last glacé cherry into place and stood expectantly. "Well poor Darby Burt is in hospital."

"Whatever is the matter with him, he always seems such a

tough little guy." Louie pictured Darby in her mind, always full of life and fun, he was very popular with everyone especially the ladies; he was a farmer and breeder of horses and was a very capable rider. "Has he come off a horse?"

"No, it seems that he took a young lady out and I suppose he got a bit fresh with her, so she whipped a cut throat razor out of her pocket and he nearly lost a part of his anatomy. I really should not laugh. Poor old Darby."

"Well any more hanky panky and someone else I could mention could get the same treatment." At this stage Janey exploded with laughter. "You have made me feel so much better" said Louie, wiping her eyes, "do you think we should visit Darby in hospital or would he feel embarrassed?"

"Not Darby. I am sure he would love to see you. Charlie and I intend to go."

The party went with a swing, no one would have guessed there was discord in the Hutt household, but later in the afternoon as the guests were departing, Sally came down from the nursery looking very concerned. Edwin was having an asthma attack and was very poorly.

Louie telephoned Dr. Pullen who lost no time in motoring to Langford. After spending some time with Edwin he joined Algy and Louie for a cup of tea. "I have been wondering," he said at last. "Would it be possible to take him to the sea and see if the sea air would do him good. I really am at a loss, could you get away even for a fortnight?"

"Yes," Algy answered without hesitation, anxious to redeem himself in Louie's estimation. He turned to face her. "Shall we go to Weymouth?"

So it was arranged. Louie rang the Hotel Burden that very afternoon and booked rooms for the day after tomorrow providing Edwin would be over his attack and well enough to travel. It was decided to take Edwin and Doreen but leave Janet with Sally and it was arranged that Zipora would stay with the girls at the farm each night.

I will ask the village constable to keep an extra vigil, thought Louie. She wondered if she should teach Zipora to shoot and leave Algy's gun under her bed, remembering the happenings when Algy went to Shropshire but she decided against it. *They say lightening never strikes twice in the same place,* she thought.

Janey promised to visit most days and would take charge of Janet on Sally's half day, though Louie had a fair idea that Sally would very likely stay with Janey and Janet. She was very fond of Janey and would probably rather have nursery tea with her than go home to her parents.

When Louie told Henrietta on the 'phone of their planned holiday, the old lady asked if there would be a possibility of her brother Wiliam Parson Guy going with them. "He has been so depressed of late," she said. They lived together, now he had retired from his farm, in a very nice house in the middle of Headington. "I think he misses the farm," she said. "He walks up to Barton every day and just stares at the old place. If only he could get away I am sure it would do him good and you know how he loves the children."

"But what about you," said Louie. "I will be alright. I am happy to be on my own. I am too old for travelling now." Louie noticed that she had become very frail of late. So it was settled that they pick old William up and take him with them. Louie made another reservation at the hotel.

The next day Edwin seemed better so the preparation and packing went ahead at fever pitch, but in spite of this, the sight of Cissy in Algy's arms still haunted Louie and she could not look at either of them without seeing vividly in her mind the scene that had confronted her in the kitchen the previous morning, but she was determined to put it behind her for now and make sure everything would be normal and the holiday enjoyed by all.

With much luggage strapped firmly to the luggage rack at the back of the car they headed for Headington. William was waiting at the window and soon appeared at the front door with his portmanteau, sporting his best suit, which smelt very noticeably of mothballs, and a broad grin.

"This is good of you to take me, I have never been to the sea," he confessed. He turned to hug Henrietta. "I wish you were coming old dear."

"Get on with you, you need to get away from my nagging for a while." Her watery old eyes were streaming with tears as she kissed the children. Louie was loathe to hustle them all into the car but knew it was a long journey and Algy would be anxious to get started. William had elected to sit in the back with the children and kept up a constant dialogue with them all the way, hardly pausing for breath.

They reached Weymouth and Algy drove slowly along the front. The excitement knew no bounds, William repeating, "Well I never did," at regular intervals and the children were standing up and staring out of the window. Edwin was six years old now, and very grown up for his years. A governess had been employed to teach them. Mrs. Jaggers came every day from the village. They were allowed to come down from the nursery to have their meals with their parents so Louie was confident they would behave well at the hotel. They were never allowed to talk at the table. "Children should be seen but not heard," Algy would say.

When they came down to breakfast the next morning, holding tightly to Louie's hand, the resplendent dining room with guests sitting at separate tables and waiters everywhere was so much to take in. Edwin whispered to Louie, asking why they could not all sit at one table, when he spotted Algy and William already sitting at a table by the window and without waiting for her to answer ran to them and allowed himself to be seated next to Uncle William, by a hovering waiter.

The food was delicious and so much to choose from, but William was adamant, "I'll just have two boiled eggs," he said. "I always have two boiled eggs and I don't want to confuse my stomach."

"Well I am going to confuse mine," said Algy. "I really fancy the kidneys," Two lightly boiled eggs were placed before William and he cut his buttered toast into neat fingers.

Louie remembered Henrietta saying he had been to the dentist and had some false teeth fitted but she could hardly believe her ears when he started eating his breakfast, his jaws made such a loud clicking noise that guests from nearby tables cast enquiring glances in their direction, but he champed away quite oblivious. Edwin stared at him transfixed and got as far as saying, "Mummy, why...?" when Louie quickly gave him a 'ssh' and a look and to her relief he went on with his breakfast,

It was a sunny June morning with just a gentle breeze and the view from the hotel window was unforgettable. William was enthralled. A scattering of people already on the sands and walking on the promenade.

A large vessel appeared on the horizon and was steaming towards Weymouth. "That's a banana boat," the waiter told them, "you can see it being unloaded later this morning if you go down to the harbour, the children would like that."

"Not just the children, I think we all would" replied Algy, he was looking at William who was thrilled at the thought of that boat unloading bananas from who knows where. The thought of that long sea voyage fired his imagination and he even refused a second cup of coffee in his haste to go down to the harbour.

Louie decided not to go as she wanted to 'phone Lower Farm and also have a word with Henrietta, knowing she would want to know if her brother was alright. Sally took the 'phone and assured Louie everything was fine and Janet was as good as gold. Henrietta was so pleased to hear Louie's voice and to hear William was enjoying himself. Now for some shopping, thought Louie, while I am on my own.

The afternoon was spent on the sands and paddling in the sea. Old William was in his second childhood helping the children to make sand castles, the tide had gone out leaving a swathe of smooth sand and the older children were drawing pictures in it. Edwin was holding his sister's hand, bare foot they ran in and out of the sea, Doreen's skirt tucked into her knickers, and picked up shells and pebbles. Algy had fallen asleep in his deck chair with his handkerchief knotted at four corners on his head. William and Louie were chatting idly away while Louie was turning the heel on the sock she was knitting, she was not a good knitter and never attempted anything more advanced than socks.

"You know Louie, that was a real thrill to see that boat this morning, I have always wanted to ride in a boat. When you are young enough to do these things you are too busy getting a living and when you get old you somehow do not bother, so I don't suppose I ever will now."

"To tell you the truth, I never have either," said Louie and resolved to remedy the situation. She had seen pleasure boats alongside a jetty filling with passengers that morning and as soon as she could get Algy on his own suggested that they go for a trip. He was thrilled at the prospect and the very next morning to the delight of William they were waiting to board a smartly painted pleasure boat and the placards informing them they would go to Lulworth Cove and spend an hour on the delightful little beach before the voyage home. The sky was blue and cloudless and there was just a slight breeze.

They were helped aboard by the skipper, a tall handsome man, bearded, bright blue eyes and a twinkling smile. The very sight of him filled Louie with confidence, she felt she could trust him with her life and that of her family, only Doreen never loosened the grip on her father's hand and scrambled on to his lap as soon as they took their seats.

The voyage was so smooth and the passengers were in great spirits. There were screams and nervous laughter when the skipper announced he was going home now, pretending he was going to leave them stranded in the cove but when he saw Edwin's worried little face he came back and gave the little lad a hug and assured him he was only joking. Then, a picnic lunch the hotel had packed for them and having had little time to explore the cove, the skipper was hustling them aboard for the homeward journey.

Louie noticed the wind had increased considerably and some

black clouds had gathered overhead and she guessed this was the reason for their short stay. As soon as the little vessel had passed through the opening to the cove and into the open sea she knew they were not going to have a very smooth voyage back to Weymouth and putting her arm round Edwin drew him close to her. A daunting thought struck her that she could not swim, the only time that she had tried was when she was about twelve years old and she went to Cromer with an aunt and had to be rescued with terrible cramp from the cold North Sea. She would never forget that experience and had no ambitions to go swimming or of trying to swim again.

The little craft chugged relentlessly on through the waves and already one or two passengers were leaning over the sides disposing of their half digested picnic lunches. Algy was next, then William. Louie grabbed Doreen and held on tight to the two children, hoping against hope that she would not follow suit, but feeling a distinct queezy feeling in the pit of her stomach. William finally stood up gripping the rail, his face ashen. "They have gone!" he gasped. Louie realised that the bottom plate of his precious false teeth was by now on the ocean bed quite irretrievable.

Algy was sitting back in his seat looking very pale but he helped the old man to sit down and assured him they would soon get him some more, "but if you are going to do it again for goodness sake take the others out first." Louie looked across at the skipper, hoping to find some comfort from his calm profile and wondered if he really was anxious. Little did she know he was anything but calm, in fact he was extremely worried though he dared not show it. The storm had come on so quickly and with such ferocity all he could do was to hope it would abate at the same speed.

"Are you feeling any better?" Louie asked William. "Just a little" he said feebly "but I'll tell you something Louie, I am not too keen on this boating lark. I have tried it now but if I get back safely I will not be in a hurry to do it again." Looking round at the other passengers Louie wondered how many of them would be of the same opinion. She patted his arm and smiled at him. "We will soon be back," she said with more assurance than she felt.

It seemed like an eternity when at last Louie wondered if it was her imagination or was the wind dropping slightly, the rain was certainly easing off a little. The skipper's voice boomed out: "I think the worst is over folks, we will soon be home."

As they stepped on to the jetty Louie turned and took the skipper's hand, "Thank you for getting us back safely." Then everyone of the bedraggled little party crowded round to thank him and praise him for his courage. Edwin was last, he looked up at the weather beaten face and holding out his hand said, "Thank you, I enjoyed it very much. I am going to be a sailor when I grow up." Algy and the skipper exchanged glances and as Edwin ran off, Algy said, "He really did enjoy it, he was not even seasick."

Louie wondered if she should get a doctor to have a look at William, he was quite an age to endure such an experience, but Algy summoned a taxi to take them back to the hotel and William assured them he would be fine after a hot bath and a good night's sleep, which proved to be the case. The next morning after breakfast Louie took William into the town in search of a dentist and Algy agreed to take the children to the beach to watch the Punch and Judy show. He soon got tired of watching Punch beating poor old Judy, however, and told the children he would go and sit on a seat on the promenade nearby and left them to shriek at the wicked Punch with the other children. Edwin asked him if he would look after his coat, it was a bit nippy when they started out and Louie insisted he wear a coat, it was new and Harris Tweed, which really was too warm for the time of year.

Doreen soon got tired of the Punch and Judy show, finding it difficult to understand the dialogue with the strange sounding voice and wandered off. Some distance away a sailor was sitting on a deck chair. She had heard someone say it was good luck to touch a sailor's collar. She walked towards him, he was backing to her and did not hear her approach but when she daringly put her hand gently on his collar he instinctively swung round, so startling Doreen that she fell backwards in the sand and gave a little startled cry. "I only wanted to touch your collar for good luck," she wimpered. The sailor laughed, it was not the first time someone had touched his collar hoping to become lucky, but never one so young. He took her hand and spoke gently to her and soon she was sitting on the sand by his side and talking happily to this stranger. He told her he had a little daughter and missed her very much when he was at sea.

Edwin, so absorbed in the show, had not missed his sister until the end, then he went in search of her. The little crowd had dispersed and still no sign of Doreen so he decided to go and tell his father. He ran up the steps to the promenade and found him on the nearest seat fast asleep in the morning sunshine. Edwin stood by him for a moment wondering whether to wake him when a thought struck the little lad. *My coat!* It was not on his father's lap, in fact it was nowhere to be seen. He ran to the sleeping man and tapped timidly but urgently on his leg.

Algy woke with a start, "Where am I?" he murmured, then caught sight of Edwin's worried little face. "What is it Edwin?" Tears started to flow down his pale cheeks. "I can't find Doreen, please help me Daddy and where is my coat?" At that moment Louie and William came towards them, "The little devil has lost Doreen," Algy stormed. Edwin ran to his mother "and Daddy has lost my new coat." Louie took his hand and hurried him down the steps to the beach. "I don't think she will have left the sands," she said. "You go that way Algy, William would you wait here in case she comes back." She knew the old man would be tired after his jaunt round the town.

She started off at a run, pulling Edwin along with her, they searched along the scattering of holiday makers asking many if they had seen a little girl on her own, but nobody had. They were nearly at the end of the bay now and Louie was frantic with worry, but trying not to show it for Edwin's sake. There was one more deck chair at the very far end of the bay, too distant to see the occupant clearly. "She can't have come this far, perhaps she went the other way and Daddy has found her."

But Edwin pulled her on, "Let's make sure Mummy." They ran on towards the solitary deckchair and could now make out something or someone beside the chair. Could it be Doreen? Louie was running so fast Edwin was having difficulty in keeping up with her. Then in unison they both gasped, "it is Doreen." She was sitting on the sand beside the sailor chatting happily. The sailor stood up. "Oh please don't move," Louie bent down and hugged her daughter, tears of relief running down her face. "We have hunted everywhere, I was so worried."

The sailor's eyes were full of compassion. "I am so sorry, I had no idea, I so enjoyed talking to Doreen I lost all track of time. I must get back to the submarine," he said as he folded up his deckchair.

The mention of submarine made Edwin look up at the sailor, eyes shining, "I have never seen a submarine."

"Well if you can persuade your Mummy and Daddy to bring you down to the harbour in the morning you shall come aboard, but don't be late, we sail at noon." He turned to Louie. "We shall be on manoeuvres and I will be away for some time, the name is Bob by the way," he said, holding out his hand to shake Louie's. "I must rush but hope to see you in the morning."

Louie hurried back along the sands to find Algy and William and set their minds at rest. Doreen, quite unconcerned, trotting along beside them. They were waiting by the Punch and Judy booth. Doreen ran to her father. "I am sorry Daddy, I only wanted to touch his collar for good luck."

"What is she talking about?" said Algy as Louie and Edwin caught up with them. Louie explained about the sailor and told them about the invitation to show them inside the submarine.

Please may we go, Daddy," Edwin pleaded. "I think Bob will be disappointed if we don't."

"I think Edwin will be very disappointed if we don't," said Louie.

"Well I suppose I will have to make it up to him for losing his coat. Someone must have stolen it. I suppose we should report it to the police."

"I think someone needed it very badly, they must have been desperate to steal in broad daylight from a man your size," Louie teased.

"I'm blowed if I would want to," said William in mock seriousness.

Algy was proud of his physique and was flattered by the remark. "You shall have a new coat," he promised Edwin, "and I don't see that I can refuse to take you to see the submarine. I have never seen one myself. Edwin's excitement knew no bounds when the little party left the hotel after breakfast to walk to the harbour. William assured them he could manage the walk, he was almost as excited as Edwin. "Wait 'till I tell the folks back home that I have seen a submarine." Like himself, very few of his friends had even seen the sea.

Louie introduced Bob to Algy and William. "I am so glad you could come," he said. "I have permission to show you aboard.

"I will wait here with Doreen." Louie headed for a nearby seat, she could not account for the way she felt at the sight of the submarine, a cold chill went down her spine, to her it had a menacing look and she feared for the crew and Bob the handsome sailor they had all befriended. This is silly she said to herself, but I just don't think I like submarines.

When the menfolk returned accompanied by Bob, they exchanged addresses and promised to write. Louie was surprised at feeling such a close affinity on so short an acquaintance. On the way home, Edwin confided to Louie "when I grow up and join the navy I shall not go in a submarine, but it was nice to see inside."

Louie rang Lower Farm each day and all was well but she found herself hankering to go home but she said nothing to the others, they were all enjoying themselves so much, especially William and up 'till now Edwin had not had an asthma attack.

That afternoon Algy suggested a char-a-banc ride, one was going to Osminton Mill and he knew Louie had so enjoyed going there on their belated honeymoon. They boarded the char-a-banc after lunch, the weather was fine and the hood was down. They sat along the back seat, Louie produced a bag of barley sugar "good for travel sickness," she said.

"We are not going to Scotland," said Algy, taking one all the same.

The seats were filling up, a rather elderly couple looked at the narrow passage between the seats and sat down in the front ones. Then a very slim gentleman sat directly behind them, his wife following in his wake except that being decidedly overweight she found herself firmly stuck. Her husband scrambled up from his seat with a look on his face denoting embarrassment and anger rolled into one. The more he pulled the firmer the poor lady was fixed. Louie looked at Edwin who was trying not to laugh but she knew that any minute he would not contain himself and she grabbed the handkerchief from Algy's top pocket and handed it to the little lad with a 'don't you dare' look on her face, and he quickly buried his face in it.

William was doing his best to keep a straight face but not succeeding very well at the sight of the extremely plump lady with her posterior firmly ensconced being assisted by her husband, who as Algy afterwards remarked, 'did not look as if he could pull the skin off a rice pudding'.

"I had better go and help," he said. Trying desperately to keep a straight face he walked up the aisle; the husband gladly stood aside.

"I think I had better try lifting you." He put his arms around the trapped lady and as he heaved her skywards he broke wind with such ferocity that everyone on the char-a-banc, without exception, heard it. Edwin, who had been on the verge of laughing out loud could contain it no longer. His infectious laughter did nothing to curb the pent up amusement of the passengers and soon they were following his lead uproariously. Algy, red in the face but victorious, held the good lady aloft and gently lowered her into the seat beside her relieved better half. The driver watched this feat of strength in amazement and was sorely tempted to ask Algy to give a swing on the starting handle to start the engine, but thankful to be able to get on the road he managed it himself and they were soon on their way. Everyone was by now in a merry mood even the elderly couple sitting in the front offered to relinquish their seats on the homeward journey. William, wiping the laughter tears from his eyes, whispered to Louie that he hadn't enjoyed himself so much for years.

They drove through the lovely Dorset countryside to the famous Osminton Mill where a delicious cream tea awaited them.

The holiday on the whole had been a success and it was now time to go home. Algy, anxious to redeem himself in Louie's affections, had been on his best behaviour apart from the odd indiscretion and Louie admitted to herself that she was feeling a little less bitter towards him.

He snapped the last suitcase shut and turned to her, "Do you realise Louie, that Edwin has not had one bout of asthma since we came?"

"No and he is looking quite bonny. I think we must do this more often but just now I am glad to be going home. I miss Janet and am sure she will be missing us by now."

"I'll go and rustle old William up and we will get on our way."

Algy was feeling homesick too but did not mention the fact and if the truth were known William was not sorry to be going home, much as he had loved being with the children and had clearly enjoyed every minute of the holiday.

Algy was soon back in the farmyard checking on the animals and pleased to see the men but was a little reticent about coming face to face with Cissy. He also knew that Louie would be watching him more closely in the future and he fervently wished the girl need not be there waiting at table or handing round afternoon tea, looking youthful and provocative in her black dress and dainty lace trimmed apron. However, he greeted her with a curt nod and a barely audible, "Cissy."

Louie was in the bedroom unpacking the cases when there was a gentle tap on the door, it was Sally, her face was flushed and in spite of her apprehensive manner Louie could see she was happy. "I was just trying to find your present. I am afraid Zipora will not be very pleased, there is quite a lot of washing."

"Oh here it is," she took a small parcel from the luggage and handed it to Sally. "Open it and then tell me your news, something has happened hasn't it?"

"Yes, ma'am." She opened the parcel as she spoke and gave a gasp of pleasure, "Oh thank you." It was a gold bangle. She slipped it on to her wrist and held out her arm for them both to admire it.

"Now tell me."

Louie sat down on the bed and indicated a chair. "I have been proposed to ma'am." Sally sat down, her flushed face turning a distinctly darker shade of pink.

"It is Ben, of course." Louie had noticed that she had become friendly of late to Lord Faringdon's chauffeur. His Lordship's visits to Lower Farm had been instrumental in bringing them together.

"I know I said he was 'cackhanded' and thought he was a great fool, but he is not so bad really and I think he will make a good husband".

"Do you love him Sally? He obviously loves you or he would not have asked you to marry him, but are you sure?"

Sally nodded. "As sure as I will ever be. Do you like him ma'am?"

"Yes, I do. I think at first we judged him unfairly, he was brought up in the town and towns people live different lives to country folk and have no understanding of animals and the like. I do know his Lordship is pleased with the way his driving has improved but I may not be the best judge of men, you must follow your own heart. Have you said 'Yes'?"

Sally nodded. "He is going to speak to my Mum and Dad next

100

week and on my next day off we will get a ring."

"He has already asked his Lordship if we can have one of the lodges that has just become vacant and he has promised it to us, so if it is alright with you, we may not have a long engagement."

"Of course it is alright, Sally. We shall miss you terribly, but you won't be far away and promise me if you have any troubles, or ever need any help, you will come to me."

Discussing Sally's replacement with Algy, it was decided not to employ another nursemaid as Janet was nearly three and would soon be joining Edwin and Doreen for lessons with the governess. So a farmer's daughter called June Crowley was finally employed as a mother's help. She was a treasure, just as Sally had been. The fact that she had been brought up on a farm had been a good training and she could turn her hand to anything. She was wonderful with the children, who Louie was pleased to see soon became very fond of her. *As long as Algy does not become too fond of her,* she thought ruefully and wondered, though he appeared distant towards Cissy, what his true feelings were. She also knew that she would never feel at ease while Cissy still worked for them. Then Janey said her parlour maid would be leaving and she would have to find another and asked Louie if she would consider letting her have Cissy if she would agree to come to Buscot.

Although it would mean training another maid, it was the perfect solution, and she said she would be willing if Cissy and her parents agreed. "I don't think I will have any trouble with Charlie," said Janey in answer to Louie's query. "You know how shy he is with women and he was so angry with Algy I really can't see him following in his footsteps." So, it was settled, Louie was sure Algy was pleased to see Cissy go and the atmosphere became less strained. Louie did not think she would ever feel quite the same about him but at least not seeing Cissy every day made it easier to forget.

When she interviewed girls to take Cissy's place, she carefully chose the least attractive of the applicants, who happily did appear to be the best suited for the job.

Algy was secretly amused when he saw the new recruit and guessed at Louie's motive. What she lacked in physical attraction however, her disposition more than compensated for and Louie knew she would fit in well at Lower Farm. Her name was Brenda and she proved to be a treasure.

Edwin's asthma attacks returned as soon as he was back at the farm and by the time he was eight years old, the doctor was very concerned about him. "They say the body changes every seven years and I had hoped he would possibly improve after he was seven but this has not happened. I really think if he stays at the farm you will lose him. You said he was better when you took him to Weymouth, is there any chance that he could stay there for a time to see how he seems, there are so many things on the farm that trigger off his attacks."

"The strange thing is," said Louie, "that although he cannot get near a horse, the smell of cows seems to bring relief and often we find him in the cow shed. He discovered it for himself".

Dr. Pullen was intrigued and after more discussion he took his leave, telling them to give some thought to Weymouth. "I think the best thing we can do is to go and stay a day or two and see what ideas come to us," said Algy. "I don't think it should be a boarding school," said Louie, wondering how she could bear to be parted from him, but knowing in her heart that the doctor was right.

So the following week Algy and Louie set off to Weymouth. They decided to go by train and when they arrived, instead of staying at a hotel they chose a boarding house on the sea front, it had been recommended by the taxi-man. "If you can get in there I will guarantee you will be comfortable. Mrs. Arnold is a lovely person and renowned for her cooking." That evening the good landlady joined them in the lounge, she was plump and homely, and her hair taken back in a bun, and Louie detected sadness in her kindly brown eyes.

They told her of their mission and quandary of what to do

about Edwin. She told them she was a widow and was running the guest house to support her family. When she told them that her youngest son Reggie had a heart condition and would probably not reach maturity, Louie felt her own troubles were insignificant in comparison. After talking for a while, Mrs. Arnold became thoughtful, then she looked up, her eyes shining.

"Would you trust me with your son, he is about the same age as my Reggie and both being delicate, I think they would get on well together. Reggie goes to a private school and if he is not well some days he does not have to attend, but he likes it there and tries to go unless he is very poorly. Edwin could do the same."

"That would be just wonderful but we could not impose on you, I think you have enough troubles of your own," said Louie.

"You would be doing me a favour. My Reggie really needs a companion, his brother and sister are a lot older and have their own interests."

So it was settled and with mixed feelings they returned to Langford, sad at the thought of being parted from Edwin for a while and thankful beyond belief at their good fortune in finding Mrs. Arnold.

Algy was particularly busy on the farm, it being the lambing season, so Louie took Edwin to Oxford to buy new clothes.

When the day came for him to go, Louie took him to the station. He had insisted that he would be quite capable of travelling by train, but as he stood on the platform, such a little scrap in his new suit slightly on the large size for him to grow into, with his parting present, the latest model a Brownie No. 2 box camera in a canvas case proudly hanging from his shoulder, she began to have doubts. An elderly gentleman, sitting on a nearby seat, had been weighing up the situation and walked towards them.

"Is the little lad travelling alone?" he enquired.

"Yes, but in the charge of the guard," Louie answered. "He is going to Weymouth."

The porter was wheeling Edwin's trunk on to the platform on a trolley. "I am going there myself," said the elderly gent. "May we be travelling companions?" He smiled at Edwin.

"Yes, please," Edwin replied. When he told them he had been staying with the Kirbys in the village, Louie felt quite happy to entrust her son to this kindly gentleman.

The Kirbys lived in a beautiful manor house next to the vicarage and it transpired that their new friend was Captain Kirby's father. "I live at Nottington a little village about four miles from Weymouth," he told them. "I will make sure Edwin gets safely to his destination," he assured Louie, taking her hand and shaking it firmly as the train steamed into the station putting an end to further conversation.

"Goodbye, Muver." Edwin always called Louie 'muver'. He never mastered the 'th' and decided when he was only six that 'Mummy' sounded babyish. Louie stood on the platform until the train had steamed out of sight, tears streaming down her face, but happy in the knowledge that Edwin would be in the company of Mr Kirby, and Mrs Arnold would be at Weymouth station to meet him and had promised to telephone when he arrived.

As she walked into the station yard a tall military figure was standing by her car. She recognised Captain Kirby at once. He came towards her smiling. "Father does not like goodbyes," he said, "so I said I would go home, but seeing your car I thought I would wait to see you." He could not help noticing Louie's tear stained face but pretended not to and told her how they had enjoyed having his father to stay.

After Louie had told him about Edwin he insisted she come back to the Manor and see Helen. "She only said this morning she had not seen you for weeks."

"I bet she has seen Doreen," Louie smiled. Doreen was about the same age as his daughter Betty and they were the best of friends.

Doreen and Janet spent many happy hours playing at the Manor and Betty in turn would come to Lower Farm, so following the Captain's car the short drive to the Manor it was no surprise to see the three girls playing in the garden.

What a handsome man, thought Louie as the Captain opened her car door and put his arm round his wife who had already joined them. For such a kind, gentle man to be trained to kill seemed to Louie, wrong. She thought of Dick, who was the gentlest of men, possibly having to kill to defend his homeland, though he never spoke about it. Helen explained that her husband was on leave and going back tomorrow. "It is nice to know she has good friends," he said when Louie promised him she would visit often and Lower Farm had a welcome that she must never forget.

The garden, like Lower Farm had a high, partly ivy clad stone wall around it, keeping it sheltered. They sat on a garden seat in the morning sunshine watching the children at play and admiring the spring flowers. A maid brought a tray with coffee and home made biscuits. "I am so glad you came round" said Helen when her husband had wandered off to play with the children. "The day before Jim goes back is hard to bear, we do not talk about it but it is uppermost in our minds. I don't think I was cut out to be a soldier's wife."

"If it is any comfort, I know a little of what you are feeling. Edwin being so delicate has been very close to me and I dreaded him going away though I know it is for the best. I just hope the sea air will do him good." Conversation came to an abrupt end as the children dragged them off to see a Jenny Wren's nest they had found in the ivy.

On the Sunday after Edwin's departure, the family set off to Church as usual. The Lower Farm pew was second from the front, the Manor was first in importance and so on down the aisle. It would have been unheard of for a lady to enter Church without a hat, and newest clothes were kept back for Sundays.

A family that Louie had much admiration for were to be seen every Sunday without fail, Mother, Father and ten children, all in their Sunday best and all so well behaved. The young husband worked on the railway. Louie never knew if that had anything to do with the fact that they lived in a railway carriage, but thought it a probability. She was shown round their cosy home one day and marvelled at the delightful little place, the front garden abounded with flowers and the back was full of vegetables. She was told that they only possessed two teacups, they always shared, starting off with Father and Mother, then the two eldest and so on down the ages, they were quite happy with this arrangement, in fact they were so content with their lot that Louie felt proud to be friends with them. "Could you make use of this teaset," she said on her next visit, "I never use it".

The children were so delighted as they unpacked the pretty china. "Now we can all have tea together," said the oldest girl.

When Zipora arrived for work one Monday morning, she told Louie she was concerned about Carter Burson's wife, she was always to be seen standing by the garden gate. She would watch her five year old son Billy go to school and then come rain or shine she would stand by the gate just leaning on it for sometimes two or three hours. "She is not standing by the gate ma'am," she said. "I have never known her not to be."

"I will go over, perhaps she is not well, though Carter did not mention it."

Louie decided to go straight away before she started the butter churning. She hurried up the road and certainly there was no sign of the familiar figure. She knocked on the front door and still there was no answer. *Perhaps she has gone to the shop,* she thought, but decided to try the back door before going to the village. It was not locked so she opened it and called out, no answer. By now she really felt there was something very wrong. She went into the kitchen and noted that it was very tidy, the breakfast things had been washed up, she peeped into the living room, which though sparsely furnished was clean and tidy. It was the first time she had been in the carter's cottage.

Louie had never called Mrs. Burson by her Christian name, in fact she never knew it. "Are you upstairs, Mrs. Burson?" but all was quiet so she timidly mounted the steep staircase. The rooms looked quite normal, the beds had been made. Louie had half expected to find Mrs. Burson perhaps unwell in the big brass bedstead, but still no sign of her. *This is a nice cottage,* she thought, as she opened the door of the third bedroom, and there, to her horror, lying on the floor in a pool of blood, her lovely red hair loose about her shoulders, lay the carter's wife. Louie stood rooted to the spot. There on the floor lay a cut throat razor as it had fallen from her hand and as the name of the instrument suggested that is what she must have done.

She decided to ring the village constable first and then go down the fields and find the carter. He would be possibly working some distance away but she felt she would rather tell him herself, if only to explain about entering his house. Algy was helping the shepherd in the other direction and she knew he would not want the unpleasant duty. After telling Zipora about her sad discovery and asking her to collect Billy from school at dinner time and on no account to let him go home, she set off to find the carter. They walked back across the fields, at first in silence, then to Louie's surprise the carter was the first to speak. "Shall I tell you why this has happened ma'am?"

"Only if you would like to carter," Louie answered.

"Before I knew her she had had a child, a boy, who had been put into a home. He were a bit simple like and I did not think I could take him on. I think she pined after him. I suppose I should have had him to live with us but I could not bring myself to, I thought when we had our Billy she would be happy but though she never spoke of him I suppose it must have played on her mind." The carter wiped the cuff of his well worn jacket across his eyes, "but I never thought she was that unhappy." They had reached the farmhouse and Louie took the distraught man into the kitchen where Billy was sitting up to the table, tucking into his dinner with Zipora fussing over him like a broody hen with a newly hatched chick.

She followed Louie and the carter into the hall. "Poor little mite," she said, "he had better stay at our house until things are sorted out. He will feel at home with my brood. I be so sorry carter," she added, as she lifted her sacking apron to wipe away a tear.

"You be a good sort, Zippy, but will Stevy mind?"

"Course he won't, you know him, the more children round him the happier he is." So it was arranged the carter would come to the farm for his dinner and Zipora would take Billy under her wing for the time being.

After Zipora had gone back to the kitchen with a generous measure of brandy 'for medicinal purposes', Louie passed an even larger glass to the carter and decided a small nip might settle her own nerves.

The door of the breakfast room opened to reveal Algy's stocky figure, the sight of the carter sitting in an armchair, a glass in his hand and the decanter on the table made him stop in his tracks.

"What's going on?" he demanded before Louie could stop him. His tone was harsh and angry but when he came into the room and noticed it was the brandy decanter, it dawned on him something was wrong. "I had better go across to the cottage," he said, when he had heard of the morning's happenings and beat a hasty retreat leaving Louie to console the carter as best she could.

The brandy was now warming the cockles of his heart, and he spoke with serious concern. "Where will they bury her ma'am?"

Louie had not thought about it until now but suicides were not allowed to be buried in consecrated ground. Where did they bury them, she wondered. After a few minutes thought, she said she would go and see the vicar in the morning. "I would not want our Billy to know his mother did that when he gets older. He is too young to understand now."

"I, personally, don't see any disgrace in it. There are times in one's life any one of us could resort to it if we had the courage," she replied. The next morning Louie headed for the vicarage and was shown into the good man's sanctuary. The room was lined with books, a large kneehole desk stood in the bay of the window and two high backed leather chairs were placed invitingly one either side of a fire in an open grate.

He stood up and took Louie's hand leading her towards the fire. "This is nice to see you Louie."

"It is nice to see you vicar, though my visit this morning is not entirely a social one."

"I think I may have an idea of the purpose of your visit, it has been bothering me too. We cannot possibly bury that dear demented lady outside the churchyard. It is something I have not had to deal with before but I think I have come up with a solution; come with me." They walked across the damp grass skirting round the graves until they came to a secluded corner with a yew tree looking as though it had been there since the beginning of time. He pointed beyond it. "There would be just room for one grave beside the stone wall."

"I am sure the carter will be pleased. I will go and set his mind at rest".

It was summer holidays and Edwin had come home for a few weeks, depending on his health. He was so much better since he had been in Weymouth and was very happy there. He looked on Mrs. Arnold as his second 'Muver' and Reggie was his 'bruver' but he was pleased to be home with his sisters who in turn were delighted to have him.

It was a happy summer. Algy had fastened a rope swing to the big pear tree in the orchard and Edwin had persuaded two of the farm hands to help him erect some old barn doors into the corner of the dry stone walls of the orchard to make a play house. They called it 'Shackleway' and spent many happy hours there. At the far end of the farm forming a boundary was a mill stream very fast flowing though quite shallow in places the clear water rippling over the firm pebbly bed. The children's favourite pastime was paddling and playing, the girls with their dresses tucked into their knickers, finding pretty pebbles and shells, catching minnows and sticklebacks in jam jars which were tipped back in before the long trudge home. Sometimes Betty Kirby would join them and when the sad news came that her father had died, she spent even more time at Lower Farm and Helen's visits became more frequent. Louie was never quite sure of how Jim met his death, only that it was some tragic accident,

The children were at an age to be full of mischief and high spirits and in fact some of their misbehaviour ended with a good thrashing with a hunting crop which Algy had picked up on the farm after the hunt had passed through. It hung on the hall stand with a menacing look but it did nothing to deter them.

One of their pastimes, a bit of fun only to be indulged in when Mother and Father were out, was what they called pig racing. The orchard was completely surrounded with a drystone wall and beyond that a small paddock with a similar boundary in the corner of which was a large shed which housed a few pigs giving them the run of the paddock. On this particular occasion Algy and Louie had only been to the village though were not expected back so soon by the children. Algy, hearing strange sounds coming from the paddock went to investigate. He peered over the wall and wondered why the door of the shed was shut and the pigs inside. The man in charge of the pigs must have had reason to get them in.

As he pondered, the door flew open and out came the large white boar grunting angrily with Edwin mounted on his back followed by a saddleback sow with Doreen precariously perched screaming with laughter, then out came Janet on the back of a young gilt, but not for long, the now excited animal kicked its legs into the air and Janet landed face down in the mud. The object of the exercise was to see who could stay on longest which in this case was not Doreen who laughed so much she lost her grip though she did not have much in the first place. Edwin delightedly proclaimed himself the winner until he looked up and saw his father's angry face and knew it would be a hunting crop job!

Louie had come to look for the children and joined Algy in time to see the frolics. "Don't be too hard on them," she whispered, "you must admit it was a funny sight."

"It won't be funny if the sows lose their litters," but after a moment's thought he gave a little grin. "I must admit it was funny but the young buggers must be taught a lesson."

"Leave it to me." Louie looked at her watch. "Its milking time, you had better go." She knew Algy did not know his own strength and did not like him chastising the children even though they deserved it and she often resorted to a sharp smack, sometimes even with the dreaded crop.

She hurried them indoors and handed them over to June who on seeing the mud spattered trio, Janet with tears streaming down her face and mingling with the foul smelling mud she knew they had been up to no good and began the cleaning up process.

"I have made my mind up," said Helen one day. "On his last leave, Jim and I talked about sending Betty to boarding school. I shall miss her terribly but I think it would be good for her, there is a wonderful school called the Blue Coat School, for girls who have lost their father and she has been accepted, she is quite happy about going."

When Louie told this news to Algy in the evening his response was, "I think it is time Doreen went to school too. I feel she needs more discipline than she gets with Mrs. Jagger."

"Perhaps she could go as a weekly boarder then we would have her at weekends," said Louie.

She missed Edwin more that she would like to admit. "Can't I go to the Blue Coat School with Betty?" Doreen begged and when she saw her smart uniform she almost envied her having no Daddy.

In the middle of Witney two sisters ran a small private school with just three or four boarders and about twenty day children. Miss Gladys and Miss Winifred were strict but kind and Algy thought it would be ideal for Doreen. She could go on the train on Monday and back on Friday. So at six years old, armed with a satchel and a season ticket, she stepped on the train at Langford Station, half excited and half apprehensive, worried that she may not be able to open the carriage door when she reached Witney. There was no corridor and as she sat thinking about it she felt very alone and increasingly frightened. Suppose no one came to her rescue. She pictured herself being taken on to the end of the line and possibly her carriage being shunted into a siding and left all night. She decided to try to open the door at the next station just to reassure herself but fate came to her rescue when a middle aged couple joined her in the carriage.

She looked forward to the journey home, the walk through the churchyard and on through the Leys which was a large recreation ground with childrens' swings in one corner. It was 'a quick go on the swings' and on to stick labels on the parcels and talk to the porters before boarding the train for home. Her father and mother had always walked up to the engine at the end of a journey and said 'goodday' to the engine driver and stoker, so, shyly at first, she did the same, then she would run from the platform through the station yard and up to the top of the bridge to wave to them in a cloud of smoke as it steamed on its way. Then she would run home as fast as her legs would carry her. The first to greet her was Philip, the gardener. He would make sure he had a little job to do in the front at that time. He was one of the workers Algy took on when they moved to Lower Farm. He had never married.

"Just never found anyone as will have me," he told Louie, but he loved children and they loved him.

It was a familiar sight to see him pushing them round the garden in his wheelbarrow. Algy would grumble that he had more children in his barrow than weeds half the time but he knew better than grumble to his face, he was a good worker and the garden was his life, every tree, shrub and plant he had nurtured to perfection. He was not much of a scholar but he knew the botanical name of all the flowers. Louie and Algy were very proud of the garden. "When are you going to let me have Philip," Lord Faringdon would say on his frequent visits. "Not this week, Sir," Algy would reply, "though I swear he spends most of his time playing with the children."

"What did you think of school, Miss Doreen?" Philip asked on her first weekend.

"Not too bad, but I don't think you would like it there Philip, there is no garden at all, just a small playground. We play badminton when the day children have gone home."

Philip looked thoughtful, "and what be badminton, I'ent never heard of that."

"It is like tennis but instead of a ball you play with a shuttlecock, which is made of feathers, but I like the train ride," she added, "and I am learning to speak in French."

Philip was suitably impressed, but as the terrier ran towards her barking excitedly, he could see the joy in Doreen's face and knew she would be missing the animals. "Your Mummy is in the orchard feeding the pet lambs I expect she could do with some help."

"Oh good." Off she went with the dog at her heels.

There were four or five orphan lambs most years, sometimes even ten to be fed on the bottle. It was a time consuming job, heating the milk to lukewarm, filling the bottles then waiting for them to guzzle it down until their little tummies were almost bursting. The children adored them and dreaded the day that they were taken from the orchard to the meadow and mixed with the flock.

Carter Burson had found a housekeeper and decided to have his wife's son to live with him.

"I think I will have to marry her," he said to Louie, "it's either that or buy another bed, and now Toebags be living with us its best she shares mine."

Louie suspected she already was and agreed that marriage was the best solution. "I don't think you can keep calling him 'Toebags' Carter, hasn't he got a proper name? He must have been christened."

"No, ma'am, he have always been Toebags and he would not know himself as anything else." So Louie did not pursue the matter and Toebags he remained. He was fifteen now and Louie guessed it was not just the Carter's conscience that impelled him to have the lad to live with him. He could get a job and his wage would be a welcome contribution.

Many houses in the towns still had no sanitation, men with a cart would empty their buckets once a week. This was the job

Toebags was set to do. He had to go to Witney on the train, a journey which gave him so much pleasure after his previous institutional existence it was like being in heaven. Whatever the job might entail the thought of boarding the train to go home more than compensated. In actual fact he really enjoyed the occupation, the company of the other men, even though they pulled his leg unmercifully, because it gave him a feeling of being wanted. He did not notice that they allocated him the houses with the largest family.

There was a row of almshouses just behind the church, these were built for elderly widows to occupy in their declining years. Toebags was happy, these buckets were not so heavy, being only one person to a house. He went whistling up the path. He passed the time of day with the elderly occupant as she stood in the doorway. "Where be the bucket?" enquired the foreman, noticing that Toebags was as he thought empty handed.

"She have only done one so it wasn't worth bringing it," he said tossing the one nonchalantly into the cart.

"You dirty little bugger," the foreman exclaimed.

"No sir, she is a clean old girl, her house be spotless."

"Well you ain't setting aside of me on the cart, you will have to walk."

When Janet was five it was decided that she should join Doreen at the Miss Walkers school as Mrs. Jaggers was not in good health and anxious to retire. She felt very grown up and though her little legs got very tired walking to the station she loved it on the train. Doreen, now quite a confident and seasoned traveller, used to choose an empty carriage and spend part of the journey doing acrobats holding on to the luggage rack or standing on her head on the seats, mischievous behaviour that Janet was not slow to emulate.

There were machines on the platform which dispensed bars of Nestles Chocolate or Frys Cream when you inserted a penny. There were other machines for the purchase of cigarettes, 'Wills Woodbines' and 'Black Cat'. They were happy to spend their pocket money on the chocolate bars until one day for devilment, they dared to get a packet of cigarettes from the machine. One of the boys at school had boasted that he had smoked a cigarette, so not to be outdone they took some matches from the kitchen that evening and with the pretext of going to see the lambs they went across the fields far enough not to be visible from the house and with much giggling they lit the cigarettes. After a few minutes and much coughing and spluttering the laughter stopped and Janet murmured, "I have had enough," and threw the half smoked cigarette to the ground and then picked up the incriminating evidence and pushed it down a nearby rabbit hole.

Doreen followed suit and popped the remaining cigarettes and matches up the leg of her drawers, "we'll have another go tomorrow," she said as they ran home. Uncharacteristically neither of the girls did justice to their supper, causing June to mention the fact to Louie and say she hoped they were not sickening for something.

"Let's have another go at smoking," Doreen said the next day, so they ran across the fields to the same spot as before, feeling safe from prying eyes. They had failed to notice Carter Burson in the next field, but unfortunately for them he did not fail to see a column of smoke rising from behind the hedge and went to investigate. They knew he had seen them and guessed he would tell their father. They waited in trepidation all day and when the nursery door opened in the late afternoon and Algy came in they knew the game was up and had no illusions about the purpose of his visit when they saw the dreaded hunting crop in his hand.

"I didn't like it very much, anyhow," said Janet suffering a very queezy stomach as well as a painful bottom. "Just as well," said Doreen. "I put the rest of the cigs down the rabbit hole. I hope the young bunnies don't get a good thrashing for smoking." They pictured the rabbits smoking their Woodbines and their tears turned to laughter but it was back to chocolate bars at the station when they next had some pocket money.

The following year Doreen was told her Auntie Blanche had

invited her to stay at Goldpits Farm for her Easter Holidays. She did not really want to go as she was looking forward to seeing Edwin but was told he was staying at Weymouth these holidays. Her Auntie and Uncle had a two year old son whom she had not seen except for a photo of him in a sailor suit in a silver frame on the drawing room mantlepiece.

The first thing that struck her was the apple blossom. The apple trees were so covered with the delicate pink blossom it was quite dazzling against the clear blue sky. Her Uncle had been mowing the lawn but had seen their approach and was waiting on the drive to meet them. He hugged her reassuringly. "How is Louie?" were practically his first words to Algy and the anxiety in his voice made Doreen suspect all was not well with her Mother.

"Mummy is not ill, is she Daddy?" she asked as they walked towards the house.

Arthur looked questioningly at Algy, "Haven't you told her?" Algy shook his head. "Well don't you think we should?"

"Yes, I do," he answered, turning to Doreen. "Mummy is going to have a baby brother or sister for you." At that moment Auntie Blanche came out of the house with Peter and took her hand. "Come on in I have made the tea."

The house looked very small after Lower Farm but it was cosy and her Aunt was a splendid cook.

They had made a comfortable living from the farm working all the hours God sent but they still did not possess a car or telephone and the bucket 'lav' down the bottom of the garden still sufficed. The worst thing about Goldpits was the fact that there was no water supply and Arthur still had to fetch it with the horse and cart so a water closet would not have been much use anyway.

Doreen soon realised that Peter though a very handsome child was thoroughly spoilt, her uncle Arthur, unlike her father was quite gentle and never smacked him. Her aunt worshipped the ground he walked on and loved dressing him up and brushing his silky curls. Doreen was surprised to see a boy dressed in white socks, just as her aunt was quite shocked to see her dressed in grey knee length boys socks and strong leather lace up shoes. "I will have to take her to Thame and get her some white socks before Sunday," Blanche told Arthur. "I am not letting Martha and Will see her dressed like that."

Every other Sunday they went to Postcome to dine with their friends who visited them alternately. Doreen had heard so much about Martha and Will she was looking forward to the Sunday morning. When duly dressed in white socks and patent leather shoes she went into the garden to find Peter who had been dressed in a silk suit and the inevitable white socks. "He looks like a little prince." Blanche had hugged him and sent him out in the garden to play while she and Doreen changed.

Doreen called and called but there was no sign of Peter. Arthur was bringing the horse and cart round to the front. She ran towards him, "Have you seen Peter, uncle, I can't find him anywhere?"

"No, I thought he was with you." He tied the horse to the railing and joined her in the search.

"Don't worry, Doreen, he can't have gone far." He took her hand and they ran together. Behind the washhouse hidden by a privet hedge was a heap of coal and there they found him playing, quite unconcerned, as black as the ace of spades from head to foot.

Doreen had never seen her uncle lose his temper but now she could see he was not best pleased as he picked up the filthy little monster and bade her go and put the kettle on the range. "I hate not being punctual," he grumbled as they finally climbed into the cart.

Blanche and Arthur sat on the seat with Peter between them and Doreen on a cushion at the back. Arthur cracked the whip and the old horse set off at a spanking pace. She guessed her uncle was still angry with Peter who was oblivious of the trouble he had caused. As they started climbing the long steep hill which led to Postcome, the horse, as if in defiance of having to pull harder began farting with great gusto at every stride he took.

117

Doreen looked round at her aunt and uncle, their faces were expressionless, not a smile passed their lips. She did not know how to suppress her laughter and was thankful to be backing to them so that they could not see her face. She was in danger of wetting her knickers and was so relieved when they reached the top of the hill and the only sound was the clip clopping of the horse's hooves.

Her aunt broke the silence at last. "Now Doreen, you must eat up all your dinner, it is so rude to leave food, especially when you visit". Arthur smiled as he recalled he had never yet seen much left on Doreen's plate, she always enjoyed her food.

Martha and Will, or Auntie Martha and Uncle Will as Doreen was instructed to call them, were about the same age as Blanche and Arthur, they had no children and the farmhouse reflected the fact, everything very much in its place. Doreen feared for the knick-knacks when Peter started toddling around and was thankful when they were summoned to the dinner table.

The maid brought a dish with two chickens roasted to perfection and placed it at one end for Will to carve, it all looked delicious and after grace was said, 'for what we are about to receive may the Lord make us truly thankful, Amen', Doreen noticed she had been served with an extra large portion of bread sauce. She started to eat, the flavour of the sauce was so abhorent to her she almost spat it out. She looked up to see her uncle and aunt both looking at her. *You knew,* she thought, *that is why you told me not to leave anything.* She decided to eat it up quickly and get it over with but she had no sooner forced the last mouthful down than Martha passed the tureen to Blanche! "Give Doreen some more bread sauce," and another large ladle of the vile tasting sauce appeared on her plate.

After the meal the men went for a walk round the farm, Doreen hoped they would take her with them but clearly she was expected to mind her young cousin while the two women had a peaceful chat. She hated the task and longed to go home to Lower Farm but would not dare to say so. Peter was a mischievous child, having lived with him for a few days she began to wish her mother was not having a baby. *Perhaps if it is a girl it won't be so bad,* she thought.

The afternoon was spent playing with Peter and listening to Martha and Blanche discussing her adenoids, "I am sure she needs an operation," said Martha. Blanche nodded in agreement. *I hope we can soon go back to Goldpits,* she thought, and fell to wondering if the horse would make rude noises going down the hill too. Martha and Blanche tried to outdo each other with their cake making and Doreen had to admit to herself it was a truly delicious tea, then homeward bound and not a sound from the old horse all the way.

The next day Blanche told Doreen that they would walk to the post office in Tetsworth in the afternoon and telephone her mother. They took turns with Peter in his pushchair. When they reached the village, to Doreen's disappointment Blanche told her to mind Peter while she went in and telephoned, she would have so liked to speak herself and was feeling very homesick.

Just to hear her mother's voice would have been wonderful. Instead Blanche came out after a few minutes with the look of a cat that got the cream and told her, "you have got a baby brother." Doreen did not answer directly. "Are you not pleased?"

She thought of her stay at Goldpits and of the hours looking after Peter, of the afternoon when he was in a tantrum and she was so exasperated with him she smacked his bottom only to look up and see her uncle looking through the window and wishing the earth would open and swallow her up. "Yes, of course, Auntie." She knew it was not the truth; had it been a foal, calf or lamb or even a girl, it would have been different, but a baby boy did not sound so appealing.

They hurried home to tell Arthur the news, they opened a bottle of home made wine to 'wet the baby's head' and she was allowed a very small glass.

Mrs. Arthur Hutt had dedicated new bells to Tetsworth church, she was Algy's aunt and was very wealthy. They were going to have a special service to commemorate the occasion. She had one son, Jimmy, a most charming man who unfortunately was very delicate. He had serious heart trouble and a hunchback; the children loved him and he them.

The baby was a fortnight old and her Mother and Father and Janet would be coming to the service, leaving the baby in the charge of Nurse Bennett, who was installed at Lower Farm for Louie's confinement. It was arranged that Doreen could go back with them.

When Peter started playing up during the service and Doreen took him out of the church, Janet followed longing to tell her sister the happenings at Lower Farm. "Do you think we will like having a baby brother?" Janet said at last.

"Not if he is anything like Peter," Doreen replied. "He is very spoilt, he never gets a smack even when he is really naughty."

They took him by the hand, "we had better go back in".

"I am longing to go home," she confided, "though Auntie and Uncle are nice, and I have had a lovely time."

Nurse Bennett finally and reluctantly took her leave, she loved being at Lower Farm but other mothers-to-be were in need of her services. She was so proud of the new arrival and smartly dressed in her nurses uniform would push the pram up the village to show off Donald Norman. "Hurry up and have another," she said to Louie as she stepped on to the train.

"Much as we love having you I hope not, four is a good size family," Louie laughed, "but you know you are always welcome."

A rag and bone man came to the farm periodically. Louie saved the rabbit skins for him and sundry other things. He was quite a character and Algy liked to have a word if he was around when he called. This morning the sun was shining and Algy was in a good mood. "Good day, Master Smith," he greeted him.

"A grand day to be sure, Sir." He counted up the skins and put them in a bag. "I am looking for a pony for my daughter, Doreen's birthday next week, you would not think of selling your little mare?"

Algy had noticed the pony very often trotting through the village. "She would not be any use to you, Sir. She will not be ridden, she is lovely to drive, but anyone who has tried to ride her has been on the ground faster than you can spit. I could do with a bigger cart for my job so I wouldn't mind selling the whole outfit at the right price."

"Well you had better name it and perhaps we can have a deal," said Algy. After a bit of wrangling a deal was struck. He took the cash from Algy and without counting it stuffed it into his 'ass' pocket handing him back the 'luck' money which was the custom on deals with horses and ponies, then tossing the bag of rabbit skins over his shoulder, promised to deliver Peggy on the 6th July without fail. Louie had arranged a party but the pony was to be a surprise.

True to his word Mr. Smith was at Lower Farm bright and early with Peggy groomed and the cart looking like new. "I shall be sorry to part with her," he said as he patted the pony, "but I know she will have a good home here."

Doreen was ecstatic, the two girls hugged Mother and Father and Peggy in turn.

Algy gave them a lesson in driving and warning them not to go in the parts of the field where the rabbit warrens were as the pony could break a leg if it stepped down a rabbit hole. He stepped down from the little cart, and walked over to where Louie was standing. "That was a very nice thing to do," she said.

He had not told her, in case Mr. Smith changed his mind or did not deliver on time. They stood arm in arm watching the pony trotting off. "There is method in my madness," Algy laughed. "I hope to be able to borrow her when we are working at the bottom farm."

The party was a grand success, trestle tables were set up in the shade of the acacia tree on the lawn. Philip had supplied baskets of strawberries for the occasion from the garden. The girls were up at four o'clock next morning grooming Peggy and fathoming out how to harness her to the cart, a task which they had not mastered, when Carter Burson came to work at six and having to admit defeat they asked his help.

He proudly taught them the correct names for the different parts of the harness, breeching straps, cruppers etc and the correct way to fit them. They were seen driving happily round the farm. Peggy was so good that when Edwin came home from Weymouth and offered to try to ride her they thought he would have no trouble and Algy agreed to help them but Mr. Smith was not exaggerating with his expression 'you would be down on the ground faster than you could spit three times'. Edwin hit the deck at great speed and decided enough was enough. Peggy obviously did not fancy being ridden and stuck to her guns.

No one tried again but one day when Peggy was harnessed to the cart and it started to rain, the children tied her up in the dutch barn to save her getting wet. Edwin dared Doreen to sit on her back, the fact that she was tied up he presumed she would not do anything wrong. Never being able to resist a dare and not stopping to think, Doreen stepped from the cart on to the shafts, walking along them until she could get on to the pony's back. As she climbed on, all hell broke loose, Peggy reared and plunged, snorting loudly, and Doreen finally landed on the ground bruised and bleeding. Thankfully the pony and cart had come to no harm.

Edwin took his sister to the horse trough and washed her cuts and bruises with his handkerchief. "We must not let Muver or daddy know".

"No, I will say I fell down," said Doreen through her tears, "it was a silly thing to do."

"It was my fault for daring you, you could have been killed." Edwin was full of retribution, blaming himself for the incident.

Doreen, seeing how shocked he looked, pretended she was not hurting. "Let's go for a drive and forget about it," she said untying Peggy, "you can drive".

"I expect I will get asthma but just a short one." Edwin took the reins and Peggy, quite calm now, went off at the trot.

Janet was in bed at this time, suffering from a mystery stomach complaint for which there did not seem to be any satisfactory cure. The doctor advised a light diet including whey, the milk had to curdle and the whey given to poor Janet. Doreen, feeling sorry for her, gave way to her pleadings and smuggled food up to the bedroom, sometimes some green gooseberries or a stick of rhubarb stolen from the garden. Despite Doreen's ministrations Janet made a full recovery to everyone's great relief and at last normality prevailed at Lower Farm.

It was an idyllic summer, Edwin's asthma had improved from his stay at Weymouth, the attacks were less frequent. He was keen on all sports and Algy enjoyed a game of cricket with the children usually after he had mown the lawn. He would put a rope on the front of the mower and the children would pull while he pushed, it was a task that Philip was happy to relinquish. The other chore that the girls were designated was to wheel Donald about in his pram until he went to sleep. He was such a lively baby, that just as they thought he had dropped off and would be tiptoeing away, up would pop his head and back they would have to go, pushing up and down once more wanting desperately to go to play.

To Nurse Bennett's delight she was booked to come to Lower Farm again the following year. It was decided that Doreen and Janet should go to boarding school at Chipping Norton. They hated leaving the Miss Walkers, looking forward to the weekends, the play on the Leys before the train ride home.

One day they had overstayed their time riding on the swings and as they ran on to the platform the train was pulling out of the station. Knowing how worried their parents would be if they were not home at the usual time they looked at each other in dismay. When they saw amidst a flurry of smoke and steam the train pull to a stop they stood transfixed. "Go on then run, they have stopped for you," said a voice beside them. It was the porter smiling broadly. "You will have to run down on the track and under the bridge in front of the engine to get on your platform."

Their faces scarlet with exhaustion and embarrassment they

ran hand in hand. "Come on you two." The driver and stoker were standing on the footplate laughing and urging them on, several heads peered out of carriage windows to see what the hold up was and an elderly gentleman opened his carriage door and helped the girls in, the guard's whistle blew once more and they were off.

The new school was in the middle of Chipping Norton, an attractive market town on the Cotswolds. On reading the prospectus Louie was really impressed. "You will be able to learn to play tennis and there is dancing," but the girls were not impressed.

"We would rather come home at weekends," Doreen answered, "and anyhow we like it at Miss Walkers." Notwithstanding, new uniforms were bought and boarding school it was. Algy drove them over, both parents hugged them and told them to be good girls and study hard and when they came home there would be another baby. Let it not be another boy thought Doreen as a teacher escorted them to the dining room for tea.

The children were all chattering away and the new girls felt very much excluded and Doreen asked the girl sitting next to her if she would mind passing the bread and butter, she answered, "We are not allowed to pass it if you do not ask in French. Only French is spoken at table."

Doreen's heart sank, she had learnt a little at Miss Walkers but 'pass the bread and butter' was beyond her. Janet had not started French lessons, so homesick, tearful and hungry they went to bed that night resolving to learn the necessary French words which were essential for their very existence.

The next morning a small bowl of extremely lumpy porridge was placed before them. When they had finished eating it Janet whispered to Doreen, "Is this all we get," and seeing the other children getting down she nodded, "I think so."

"I hate it here."

"So do I," replied Doreen, "but there is nothing we can do about it. I think we play tennis this afternoon, that should be fun." She tried to cheer her young sister but her heart was heavy, she could see tears streaming down Janet's face as she ran off to her classroom.

When the bell rang for dinner time there was a race for the dining room, it seemed an eternity since they had eaten that small bowl of porridge. The savoury smell coming from the kitchen boded well and the children were soon sitting up expectantly but as the plates were placed before them their faces dropped and Doreen heard the girls next to her say, "the same old thing as last term." It was two extremely thin slices of corned beef and a dab of mashed potato. The girls liked corned beef but after it had been served to them every day for a week, Janet rebelled. She pushed her plate away and told the maid she could not eat any more corned beef for the time being.

Every girl within hearing stared in amazement, the maid, equally astonished, picked up the plate and headed for the kitchen. After a few minutes the head mistress emerged and strode to where Janet sat defiantly, "come with me girl". She took her hand and without another word marched her from the room.

When the door closed behind them, there was a renewed buzz of conversation mostly consisting of speculation as to what would be the outcome of Janet's little outburst. When the meal was over and Janet returned to the dining room, silence reigned and everyone waited expectantly for her to tell them what had transpired but she just tossed her head and ran to her sister who was just leaving the room. When they were alone, Doreen asked her what had happened. "I was told not to tell the others but I had a lovely dinner with the teachers and fruit salad for pudding, but I am not to do it again."

"I thought you would get the cane," said Doreen.

"So did I," Janet answered with a wry smile. The term had nearly ended when an epidemic of whooping cough hit the school. When Algy collected the girls at the end of that term he hardly recognised them. They were not able to see the new baby or get near Donald for fear of giving them the dreaded cough.

To the girls relief their parents were so distressed at the sight of them that on no account would they let them return to Chipping Norton.

Nurse Bennett held the baby Wilfred Gordon up to the dining room window for them to see. He was as different from Donald as chalk and cheese, Donald having dark eyes and brown curls, Wilfred having blond hair and blue eyes. It would be another boy grumbled Janet but both girls had to admit he was a lovely baby.

The fact that the rooks had built their nests high in the topmost branches of the elm trees that spring Algy maintained it indicated a hot dry summer. His prediction that year proved to be correct and the children enjoyed cycling round the country roads, often falling off their bikes in fits of coughing and spending many happy hours in the far meadow with the mill stream. They would drive down in the pony cart then unharness Peggy and turn her loose to graze until they were ready to go home. They did not have a watch, their tummies told them when it was teatime.

It was back to Miss Walkers school at the end of that lovely summer holiday and Edwin still spending his term time at Weymouth with his second Muver and Reggie. "I think Mrs. Arnold has found a new husband," he told Louie at the end of the term. "One of the guests is often talking to her even in the kitchen."

"Even in the kitchen?" Louie questioned.

"Well the guests never come into the kitchen and in any case they would knock first, but he comes straight in. He is very nice, even Reggie likes him and Mrs. Arnold likes him, I can tell."

Louie smiled, Edwin does not miss much, she thought. When a letter came about a month later to say she was to marry a Mr. Brownlow, Louie was not altogether surprised and wrote back without delay. After discussing it with Algy she suggested that they spend their honeymoon at Lower Farm if they had nothing fixed.

This offer was soon accepted and the happy couple arrived at Langford to everyone's approval and delight. Soon after their arrival Mrs. Arnold, now Mrs. Brownlow, explained that she would be giving up the guest house to retire into a bungalow. It had crossed Louie's mind that this might happen and though she was pleased for her Louie knew that other arrangements would have to be made for Edwin. They finally decided on a boarding school at Ramsgate. He would miss Mrs. Brownlow and Reggie very much but went off happily to his new school. Louie resolved to visit him often, remembering what had happened to the girls at Chipping Norton. She knew he would miss the animals. Even when he was at Weymouth, he and Reggie bought some white mice. They used to go on the sands and let the mice run all over them and trained them to do little tricks. This attracted a crowd of onlookers who would throw them coppers, they found it quite a lucrative pastime. Edwin brought his three mice home with him that holiday and kept them in a hutch in 'Shackleway' their playhouse in the orchard unbeknown to his parents but when term started and they all had to go to school they decided the only course of action was to let them out to fend for themselves with the result that they interbred with the native mice and strange coloured mice were seen at Lower Farm, some white with patches of brown, some brown with patches of white.

Algy was getting increasingly bad tempered and Louie felt he was working too hard. One day, on their way to Faringdon in Algy's car, as they rounded a bend there was a man on a bike ahead of them. Hearing a car the man swerved to the side of the road and cycled as near to the grass verge as it was possible to get. To Louie's horror Algy wound down the window, "You big headed bugger," he bellowed, "do you want all the bloody road?" He put his foot hard down on the accelerator and the car shot forward at such a speed, Louie was catapulted back into her seat. On recovering, she glanced back in time to see the unfortunate man fall head first on to the bank. "Algy," she gasped, "do you know who that was?"

"No and I don't care, he was all over the road." He set his jaw and drove on at great speed.

"Well you may not get your ricks thatched next year, that was

127

old George and you never even stopped to see if he was alright." Algy paled slightly, he knew no one could thatch as well as George, the ricks of hay and straw were a sight to behold, he took such a pride in his work, making a pheasant out of straw and placing it strategically on the rick.

Algy did not speak again on that journey, Louie knew he was regretting his action. She knew also that something must be done to lighten his load, he had had an operation for a duodenal ulcer and was not really over it, so Louie felt she must make allowances, but as the weeks went by and Algy's temper got worse, she made up her mind to persuade him to move to a smaller farm.

When one day June called to her notice Janet's bottom and legs—he had given the girls a thrashing for some small misdemeanour—Louie and June decided they must stay away from school for a few days until the weals had faded. This resulted in Louie making up her mind something must be done and unknown to Algy, the next morning she went into Lechlade to see an auctioneer and ask him to look for a smaller farm.

The auctioneer was sympathetic, he knew Algy very well and had on occasions been on the receiving end of his outbursts of temper if he had not managed to get a high enough price for some livestock at the weekly cattle market.

"I haven't anything suitable to rent at present," he said as he flicked through the pages. "There is a very nice farm just come up for sale though, three hundred and fifty acres, a nice farmhouse and three cottages, it is near Black Bourton."

He handed the particulars to Louie. "I doubt if we could buy," but she put them in her handbag.

On the way home she decided to go to see Janey and Charlie, knowing the baby boys would be in safe hands with June, "I have known you long enough to know there is something troubling you" said Janey. Soon Louie was telling her friend about her plan to try to persuade Algy to move, she told her about the girls wealed bottoms and the episode with George and other temper tantrums. Janey looked at her in disbelief . "I know he has got a temper but I had no idea things were this bad. You could never leave Lower Farm, Louie."

"I will hate to, of course, but something has got to be done, anyway chance would be fine thing, the agent had not got a farm on his books to let, only this one for sale." She took the particulars from her handbag, "but I don't think we would be able to buy."

They read the particulars together, "it does sound nice though, don't you think?" asked Louie.

Janey nodded, "I like the sound of the mill stream, a bit of fishing would do Algy worlds of good, it is very relaxing, perhaps that is what he needs."

"He needs something, that's for sure," said Louie, "as soon as I can catch him in a good mood I will show him these." She folded up the papers and returned them to her handbag. "I feel so much better for our chat."

When she got home it was to find the girls in tears. Donald, now two years old had somehow found a knife and while June was preoccupied momentarily, he ran into the garden, headed straight for Algy's prized asparagus bed and did his best to emulate his father, cutting the spears. The bed looked for all the world as if a wild animal had gone berserk. Algy in his rage on discovering the carnage had thrashed the girls for not looking after him. June was very upset, she said she had not asked the girls to look after him, but Mr. Hutt would not listen. Louie was more determined than ever to pursue her idea of getting a smaller farm and that evening broached the subject to Algy, telling him in no uncertain terms that they could not go on the way they were. She told him of her visit to Lechlade and about Mill Farm, Black Bourton. "We will go and see it there would be no harm in that, they may take an offer," she said. So it was arranged and the next day saw them driving towards the village of Black Bourton, on through the little village towards Bampton. About half a mile along the road they found the white gate and long drive leading up to a typical Cotswold stone farmhouse with solid stone barns to one side and stables and granaries to the other. They drove over a bridge with white railings on either side. Algy saw the clear fast running water of a brook and stopped the car. Cattle were standing in a shallow and nearer to them a heron stood poised on the water's edge.

"Look at that old molhern Louie, I bet there are trout." Algy spoke at last, he had hardly said a word on the journey. He was in a dilemma, he did not want to leave Lower Farm but the work had got on top of him lately. He started the car and drove to the house where they were met by the owner who explained that he was retiring. It was plain to see he loved the place, it was obvious too that Algy was already very taken with it and when they were shown round the house Louie found herself planning the furniture. It was nowhere near as spacious as Lower Farm but was a charming house with a welcoming feel to it.

This is ridiculous thought Louie, why are we looking at it, we can't afford to buy it. After walking round the farm and enjoying the proffered cup of tea they took their leave, promising to give an answer soon. "We should not keep them in suspense when we know we can't afford it," said Louie as they drove home.

"Well I am not so sure about that," Algy surprised her.

"You did like it then?"

He nodded. "Did you?"

"Yes, very much." She wondered if a different house and kitchen, especially the kitchen, would help to eliminate the ever recurring memory of that fateful morning.

"I will have a word with Mr. Hook this evening, he has always said he would like this farm."

"I know Mr. Hook loves the house, but he is a chapel man, would the church commissioners let to someone of a different denomination?" asked Louie doubtfully.

"He is a first rate farmer, that is well known, and must go in his favour."

However, Mr. Hook jumped at the chance to have Lower Farm and was accepted as tenant and the owners of Mill Farm, anxious to complete for a house they fancied by the sea, after much deliberation eventually accepted Algy's offer. So it was they moved to Mill Farm, Black Bourton and Louie hoped with all her heart that Algy would become easier to live with.

There was so much to learn about the workings of the new farm. The mill stream being the source of energy for grinding the corn and generating the electricity. There were three nice cottages, two in the centre of the village and one across the fields to the side of the house which the carter chose. Walter Hunt came with them from Lower Farm too and Herby occupied the third cottage. He was a widower and his daughter kept house for him. She was a very smart attractive woman in her late twenties and was to soon set tongues wagging when smart cars and well dressed gentlemen stopped at the cottage. One or two people complained to Louie but as she explained, it was nothing to do with her. "We employ her father," she explained, "and there is no denying no fault could be found in the way she keeps house for him." The cottage was a credit to her. Louie called one day to speak to Herby and she wondered how she could do so much work and still have time for hanky-panky, she had even made the loose covers on the fireside chairs really professionally.

For reasons best known to herself, Louie did not tell Algy that she had visited Herby's cottage. Deep down she did not want him to know of his daughter's goings on, she knew he would be bound to find out sooner or later. Walter living next door would sure to know and would tell him.

I will never trust him again, she thought, and was secretly glad that the village was a good mile from the farm. There was a footpath across the fields passing the back of the farm house and on to Bampton with kissing gates in the hedges, not many people used the path except the farm workers. A few would come at blackberrying time or in the autumn hoping to find some mushrooms.

The doctor was worried about Janet, she had trouble with her throat and he hoped she would not develop tuberculosis. It was decided a spell of sea air would be the best thing for her.

The air at Weston-Super-Mare was reputed to have wonderful healing qualities, resulting in some convalescent homes being built there. There was a boarding school for girls just outside Weston on a headland overlooking the sea. Louie thought it would be ideal, if a bit expensive, but as she argued when Algy grumbled about the fees, "what is money if health is at risk," so he finally agreed and Janet, after being fitted out with her new uniform was packed off to Weston-Super-Mare. Louie thought if she could increase the hens and sell the eggs it would help pay the children's school fees.

Algy was adamant about the children being well educated but it was like drawing a hind tooth to get him to pay the bill. Carter Burson's son, Billy, who had now left school, was employed to help with the poultry and pump the water. There was a hand pump connected to a well near the back door which supplied the house. It took about an hour's pumping to fill the tank in the attic. This task completed, Billy came in the house for a cooked breakfast before helping Louie with the chickens. Some of the hen houses were fitted with iron wheels and after the corn had been harvested a horse would pull the houses down to the cornfields and the hens would have food for weeks before the fields had to be ploughed.

When Edwin came home from his school at Ramsgate, Louie felt that all was not well, he did not complain but he was not his usual merry little self and it took some time to wheedle the truth out of him. The older boys and prefects picked on the new boys and made them fag for them, this entailed cleaning their shoes and keeping their rooms tidy. It was the understood thing in boarding schools. Edwin knew that and was prepared to do his share but he had a bit of spirit and would only stand so much which resulted in a flogging all too often.

Louie and Algy went to see Mr. Stileman who was the head master of Burford Grammar School and were impressed by both the master and the school. It was a fine old building, built in the same lovely mellow cotswold stone as the rest of the picturesque little town. Louie fervently hoped Mr. Stileman would agree to take Edwin. After much discussion it was agreed that he should start the next term. In the holidays Edwin had made a pet of a young jackdaw and taught it to say a few words. When he went for his interview he asked Mr. Stileman if it would be possible for 'Jack' to come with him. To Edwin's delight Mr. Stileman relented and 'Jack' became as much a part of the school as the pupils themselves and his vocabulary very much improved with his Grammar School education. He would sit on the sill outside the window of Edwin's classroom and join the boys with "good morning, Sir," when a master entered the room.

Herby was a real character, the children got on well with him, Algy swore at him continually but he never took offence.

The raspberries and blackcurrants were grown in the corner of the vegetable garden in a wire frame. Janet and Doreen were picking raspberries one bright sunny morning, a few of the luscious berries finding their way into their mouths, suddenly their father's voice boomed out, "Herby are you there?" The girls put down their bowls and scrambled on to the dry stone wall which surrounded the garden. On the other side was the rick yard and from their vantage point they could see Herby lying beside a rick of hay in the sunshine. "Herby you old bugger, I know you are there." He leapt to his feet but remained hidden. "He is over by the mill, Daddy," Doreen shouted sending her father in the opposite direction and giving Herby time to get to the cowshed where he should have been working. "You be good gals," he said as he hurried past them, "even if you do tell fibs."

Jimmy Clack came from Clanfield, a village about two miles away, on his bike every day. He was employed to do the hedges and ditches. On Sundays he preached at the chapel. He would sit in the granary to have his sandwiches at dinner time and the children were sent out with a plate of pudding for him. Algy was careful to watch his language in his presence. When he first started working at Mill Farm, Algy let rip at him with what was for him a mild obscenity, to be told by Jimmy in no uncertain terms that if he ever swore at him again he would leave his employ. Knowing what a good worker he was Algy made sure he never did, it was always "Jimmy, my boy."

June Cowley had to go home to look after her mother, now an invalid and a new mother's help was employed, called Maggy, a rather straight laced girl. The older children did not like her, they did not like the way she treated the two little boys. In front of their parents she was all sweetness and light but in the nursery she would feed little Wilfred with a bowl of bread and milk for his breakfast and sit him on the floor daring him to move. The girls would get him up and play with him when her back was turned, sitting him down quickly when they heard her footsteps on the stairs. There was no way she could keep Donald still though. He was full of life and mischief, there was no way he would have sat still.

Edwin was doing well at Burford School so Algy and Louie decided to send Doreen there now she was nine. There were no girl boarders at the school but a Mrs. Pearman, who was a widow with two sons at the grammar school allowed the girls to board at her lovely home and treated them with the same devotion as her own sons. It was a happy household. Jack was the eldest boy, tall and fair and so very handsome. Bob was dark but equally good looking in a different way. He was a real tease and Doreen was never quite sure if he was pulling her leg. Being the youngest of the three girls she came in for quite a lot of that but they were patient with her too. At weekends they would go for long walks or cycle rides in the surrounding countryside.

The River Windrush runs through the town at the bottom of the hill and it was a favourite walk along the banks looking for moorhens nests and watching the kingfishers darting flight as they followed the bends of the river. The nature walks were a great joy to Doreen. Once a week her form mistress, Miss Bradwell, would line them up in a crocodile, two and two, holding hands. They took a notebook and pencil and walked through the countryside sketching and making notes about the flora and fauna.

134

Most of the girls were from farming families and already knew at least the most common species but never stopped learning and loved being out in the fresh air.

The farm was not paying as it should and contrary to Louie's hopes that Algy's temper would decrease with a smaller farm his rages persisted. She worked ever harder with the poultry. One day she caught Billy sucking eggs, she knew there was no need for this as he had a good breakfast at the farm and he admitted his stepmother gave him good food. She threatened that if he did it again it would be the sack, though she had a fair idea he still had the odd one but was more careful about hiding the shells. She kept the knowledge to herself knowing it would only send Algy into a rage and he would be sure to sack the boy and Louie was glad to have his help. Like his half brother, 'Toebags', the poor lad was twopence short of a shilling and it would be difficult, if not impossible, for him to find employment.

As time went on it became clear to Louie that Algy had no intention of paying Janet's school fees, so after much deliberation she decided to go to the Department of Education in Oxford and see if they would put a school bus on for Burford Grammar School then all the children could go daily. She felt very nervous as she was shown into the office of the head of department but he soon put her at her ease and they had a pleasant chat. I will talk it over with my colleagues and let you know he said as he shook hands with her, but don't hold out too much hope as there may not be enough children to fill a bus from that area.

When the telephone rang a few days later and she recognised the voice of the head of the department, she could hardly wait for his reply. We have discussed your request he said and we feel we cannot undertake this procedure, however, if you can find enough pupils to fill a coach and you put it on yourself I am sure that would be alright by us."

"I will see what I can do," she anwered feeling slightly dismayed. As she replaced the receiver she resolved to get this bus running 'come hail or high water'.

She made a list of friends and neighbours and after making numerous 'phone calls it became clear that she would be able to fill a coach. The next day she went to Witney to see a Mr. Backs who had a small coach business. He readily agreed to supply this service and the next term Mrs. Hutt's coach as it was called, was at the drive gate to pick up Louie's three children.

Janet's throat trouble had cleared up and proved not to be tuberculosis.

Doreen was sorry to leave Mrs. Pearmans but was thrilled at the thought of being with the animals and able to help her mother with the poultry in the evenings and at weekends.

At this time Algy was having trouble with selling the milk and after an unsuccessful trip to London he decided to rear calves with it so he bought sixty calves and a separator. The children had to help in this new venture, taking it in turns to turn the handle of the machine which separated the milk from the cream and each calf was individually fed with milk from a bucket, then it was a mad dash to change into school uniform and run down the half mile drive to catch the 'bus. Louie contributed to the project by making the cream into butter and many pounds were despatched each week to nearby shops and hotels.

Donald was missing!

Maggy had been helping with the butter churning and failed to notice him slip away.

Algy was away in the fields and there were no men near the buildings. After searching the house to no avail Louie and Maggy started looking outside but their calls were only answered by echoes and there was no sign of the little boy. Terror struck Louie's heart as she ran towards the mill stream. A small child could easily drown in the brook but the mill stream was very deep and full of reeds, to reach it there was a plank bridge spanning the brook just by the mill wheel.

When the wheel was not in use the water was shallow but when it was turning it was not only fast flowing but quite deep. As Louie looked down, to her relief there was Donald wading waist deep in the water. Had the mill wheel been working he would have been swept away and undoubtedly drowned. He looked up and saw his mother, as he did so he lost his balance and toppled over into the water disappearing beneath the surface. Her frenzied screams brought Maggy to the scene by which time Louie had clambered down the bank and into the water and was clutching a dripping bundle tightly to her chest and wading towards the bank. They both collapsed on to the grass with tears of relief streaming down their faces as they comforted little Donald. "I don't think it would be a good idea to tell my husband. There is no need to worry him". Maggy readily agreed to keep her secret, knowing she was partly to blame and knowing how near it had been to a tragedy.

On the Bampton side of the farm, the land adjoined that of a wealthy neighbour who farmed more for fun, not needing to make a living. He was what Algy called a gentleman farmer, though he watched with interest, albeit from behind hedges, the goings on. He used tractors on the farm instead of horses which Algy thought was a huge joke and had bets with his friends as to how long the farm would still be in business. He had read about a machine being invented called a combine harvester but 'pooh poohed' the idea. That will never work, he was quite sure. When he looked through the hedge one day and saw this large rather cumbersome machine being driven on to a field of ripened wheat he could hardly believe his eyes. He stood watching and listening as the men from Castle Farm were given instructions by engineers on how to work this remarkable feat of engineering. It will never catch on he muttered as he walked home, but he telephoned Charlie and one or two other friends who were soon driving in to Mill Farm to see for themselves what a combine harvester looked like and if it really performed the miracle of thrashing the standing corn.

They stealthily lined themselves up along the hedge at the best vantage point. "I would reckon Master Diamond has got more money than sense," said Algy.

Charlie nodded, "Maybe, but only time will tell."

Herby had joined the onlookers, "gert big thing 'ent it", he remarked in a hushed voice.

"What do 'e think Carter Burson. After all, it would be you as would have to work it if the master gets one."

"I don't think as ever he will somehow," said the carter, "but I must admit it is a clever idea." They stood peering through the hedge and smoking their pipes, not realising that the puffs of smoke rising above the hedge had given their presence away and Mr. Diamond walked across the field towards them.

"Good afternoon, Mr. Hutt." Algy felt rather foolish.

"Good afternon, Mr. Diamond," he replied. "I see you are interested in my combine harvester. You are welcome to come and have a look, and bring your friends, of course." He was pleased to show off his new toy knowing it would be a talking point for miles around.

Louie was working hard with the poultry but it was an uphill battle. A neighbouring farmer on the other side of the farm was very keen on fox hunting and encouraged the foxes to breed on his farm for the pleasure of hunting.

They were a very nice family and Algy and Louie were good friends with them but Algy had forbidden the hunt to step one foot on his land after they had once galloped over a field of sown wheat. Now after some devastating happenings in Louie's chicken runs he was more anti-hunt than ever and took the shotgun to the foxes taking care that his neighbour did not find out. Still the chickens disappeared and Louie was sure someone was helping themselves, this time a human 'fox'.

There were many species of fowl at Mill Farm, wild duck in abundance, geese, turkeys and guinea-fowl. The guinea-fowl perched in a large ash tree at night and were excellent guards, anyone or anything about the place at night and they would start their 'come back, come back' sound, screeching loudly. Doreen dreaded being wakened by her father. "Come on, Doreen, there is someone outside."

In dressing gown and 'welly' boots she would go, torch in hand. "You go to the orchard and I will go to the rick yard."

What will I do if I do see someone, she thought, desperately hoping she would not. Every bush or hedge she imagined someone was lurking and longed to be back safely in her warm bed.

Louie told the local police constable about the missing chickens. He would come to the farm after dark, first he would come to the farmhouse, enjoy to the full the hospitality of the house, then he would say he would go and check that there was no one about. On his way home he would help himself to a chicken for his Sunday dinner, so there was more than one fox, human and otherwise, enjoying the proceeds of Louie's hard work.

Edwin's asthma excluded him from working with the poultry and Janet preferred helping Maggy with the two little boys, bathing them and putting them to bed, but Doreen was always happy helping her mother with rearing the baby chicks, turning the eggs in the incubators and testing them with a torch light to see if they were fertile. This was a long painstaking job and her school homework often suffered. It also suffered at lambing time when orphan lambs had to be fed, which resulted in her trying to do it on the school 'bus which was not a great success.

At this time Algy had the good fortune to inherit a house from an Aunt. It was a beautiful house called "Highfield" in the attractive village of Lane End in the Chilterns. There was a four acre paddock at the back and a tennis court which needed mowing every week. So that summer a picnic was packed each Sunday and the whole family went off in Algy's car to Lane End. Louie did not look forward to the journey with Algy blustering the car along the highways and byways, but when they arrived there was so much to do and see the time just flew. They watched the red squirrels capering about in the adjoining wood. They became very tame and were soon accepting morsels from the picnic to everyone's enjoyment. They all helped with mowing the grass and weeding the garden and before the homeward journey they would go into the greenhouse where nectarines were hanging ripe on the vine. They had never tasted them before but there was no doubt about their approval with 'umms' and 'aahs' and juice running down their chins.

The first thing Doreen would do when returning from school was to run to the meadow to see her pony, she had little time for drives but she liked to groom her and give her a cuddle. When one day she was not in her usual field she went to ask her mother which meadow she had been moved to. "I hoped I would catch you before you went to see Peggy."

Louie looked distressed. "Your father sold her today. I begged him not to but he said he did not need her now."

"But she was my pony," Doreen burst into tears, "how could he, at least he should have asked me?"

"That is what I told him but he would not listen and when I came back from collecting the eggs, Peggy had gone. I am so sorry, dear." She put her arms round Doreen and hugged her.

"I will never forgive him."

"I won't either, as long as I live."

Doreen went out to feed the lambs with so much hurt and anger inside her. When she came in for tea, her father was already sitting at the table, she did not look in his direction as she took her place at the table. She drank the cup of tea her mother passed to her but uncharacteristically ate nothing and before the meal was over, asked to be excused.

She went outside and called the four dogs. There was Bessy, a cocker spaniel, Algy's gun dog, Spot, the sheepdog, Rover, Bessy's son, who was being trained to take her place when she retired, but according to Algy was too silly to ever make a gun dog, but the children loved him. Then there was Myrtle Evershed, the terrier, the only one of the bunch allowed in the house. Louie bought her from a Mr. Evershed. She picked her from the litter and on the way home with the children holding her in turns, suggested Myrtle for her name, and the family agreed.

When they reached home and Janet held the puppy up to her father and announced this is Myrtle Evershed, daddy, Myrtle

Evershed she remained. Now adult, she was a dab hand at catching moles, she would always stand on three legs with her head on one side watching the mole hill until the moment was right to pounce, sometimes taking hours. Often she had not returned as darkness fell and it meant a search of the likely fields to find her and coax her to give up and come home.

Doreen followed the course of the brook, the dogs delightedly following at her heels, stopping where the bank was low enough for them to lap the cool clear water. It was a warm evening and dragon flies were circling above the brook showing off their brilliant colours, a water rat swam upstream and crept into a hole in the bank. She presently came to the spinney at the other end of which was the boundary of the farm, the brook continuing its winding way to Bampton. She followed the track to where a willow tree had fallen, straddling the brook to the far bank and sank down on its trunk giving way to her feelings. She knew her father would never tell her who had bought Peggy and there was a possibility she would never see her again. Rover came and sat beside her, pushing his soft body close, instinctively recognising her grief. She had decided to go home, knowing it would be time to help with the chickens, she dipped her handkerchief in the brook and washed her tear-stained face and was about to climb from the tree when she heard a twig snap and then running footsteps and heavy breathing, and into the clearing Edwin came running. "I guessed you would be here," he said as he collapsed on to the bank. The dogs appeared from nowhere to welcome him. "Muver was worried about you and she needs your help with the chickens."

"I was just coming."

Doreen joined her brother. "You should not have run, is your asthma bad? You sound dreadful."

"It is not good, today," he said, climbing to his feet. "Daddy selling Peggy has upset us all. I just don't know what made him do it".

Doreen felt guilty that her brother had walked so far to find her whilst feeling so poorly. He never complained, even though his asthma often prevented him taking part in his favourite sports. He loved playing football in spite of his ill health, and was a keen boxer, and to his pride and joy, he won the boxing prize at school.

Algy had always resented the fact that Edwin was delicate but to Louie's amazement he actually went to the prize giving that year after hearing Edwin mention that he was hopeful that he might win it. The prize was a beautifully bound book of *The Art of Boxing,* and to everyone's surprise Algy read it from cover to cover. He rarely, if ever, read a book, Daniel Defoe's *Robinson Crusoe* being the exception. *The Farmer and Stockbreeder* and the newspapers were the extent of his reading.

The following week when the children returned from school they noticed that Algy's face looked, to say the least, battered and bruised, with a decidedly black eye but they did not like to remark upon it and carefully averted their eyes at tea-time. After tea, Louie had no shortage of helpers as they followed her to the orchard to gather apples. Edwin looked at his Mother expectantly

"What happened to Daddy?" he asked.

While they were gathering the apples Louie told them of the day's happenings. On the village side of Mill Farm was a farm owned by Jimmy Watts. The Cotswold stone farmhouse was in the village flanked by a high stone wall, at the back of which beyond the farmyard ran the mill stream which continued through his fields and on to Mill Farm. It had been a particularly dry summer and there was not enough water in the stream to enable Algy to charge the electricity with the mill wheel, forcing him to purchase a diesel engine to do the job. That morning Herby told Algy that he had seen Jimmy erecting a dam in the stream. Algy was incensed. "He has no right," he stormed, and in spite of Louie pointing out that he had every right on his own farm he strode off in the direction of the mill stream. When he reached the boundary just a few yards upstream, Jimmy Watts and one of his men were putting the finishing touches to a very solid looking dam across the stream. Algy's face was scarlet with anger. "Jimmy," he hailed him, "what the devil do you think you are doing to my stream?"

Jimmy strolled nonchalantly across to where Algy was standing. "Mr. Hutt," he said calmly, "that is your stream." He pointed to Algy's side of the boundary. "This," he said, "is *my* stream and I will do what I like with it." The argument got more heated, the man helping Jimmy had come closer to watch proceedings and when he saw Algy take his coat off and roll up his sleeves he stood open mouthed in anticipation. Jimmy climbed over the fence and faced Algy. "I really don't like fighting a man so much older than myself but if you insist."

"Age, nothing," said Algy holding up his fists threateningly, but as he lunged forward his opponent, quick as a flash caught him with an uppercut to the jaw sending him staggering backwards. This so enraged Algy that barely recovered he advanced with fists flying, but Jimmy stood his ground and two more sharp jabs went home to Algy's face and very soon he slunk away muttering, "You bugger, I will get you for this," his eye already so swollen he could hardly see. Jimmy climbed back over the fence and proceeded to finish building the dam with the sure knowledge that the episode would soon be village gossip.

Louie did not need to ask what had happened, but went to the pantry with a carving knife, returning with a lump of raw steak. "Put this on it," she said, "it will bring the swelling down," but also knowing it would not help to calm his rage or make him easier to live with for the next few days.

There was, to everyone's concern, an outbreak of diptheria at Burford School and several of the children had been sent to Abingdon isolation hospital. It being such a deadly disease, prayers were said for their recovery at morning assembly and parents kept a careful watch on their children.

After the school bus had dropped the children and they started to walk up the drive, Doreen was lagging behind. "Come on, Dor," Edwin shouted.

"I can't walk very well," Doreen replied. "I feel dreadful and my head aches."

Edwin went back to her, "I expect you have got a cold coming on," he said relieving her of her satchel and taking her arm. When at last they reached home Doreen sank into a chair and held her throbbing head in her hands while Edwin went in search of their Mother. He found her in the dairy patting the butter. The look on Edwin's face told her that something was amiss and when he told her about Doreen, she lost no time in 'phoning the doctor.

"I am afraid she has got diptheria," he announced at last. "I will arrange for her to go to the isolation hospital."

"Please don't make me go there," Doreen begged. The word isolation struck fear into her heart. "Well this house is well away from the village, but do you think you could nurse her, Mrs. Hutt?" Louie agreed. "Any staff you have must not leave the house and the other children must not go to school or leave the farm."

While giving instructions he produced a hyperdermic needle from his bag and told Doreen to turn over on to her tummy. By now she felt too ill to care as the needle was pushed into her bottom. Pills and potions were produced before he took his leave promising to come again tomorrow.

Louie was instructed to hang a sheet soaked in disinfectant over the door and put a smock on before entering the room. Louie told Maggy and the daily maid but that evening as soon as it was dark, they crept from the house without a word, this saddened Louie, though she really could not blame them, but wondered how she would manage, hoping against hope that the other children would not catch it but before the end of the week was up, Edwin, Janet and Wilfred were all diagosed as having caught it.

Janet was very ill and one night Louie after sitting with her all night woke Algy in the early hours. "I don't think Janet will make it 'till morning. I think you should come and see her."

"There is no sense in me catching it," he replied. Louie made her way sadly back to Janet's bedside. She knew it made sense for him to keep away but with his daughter so very ill she wondered how he could not want to see her. She lay there so still, Louie had to feel her pulse to make sure she was still alive.

The dawn was breaking, a cockerel was crowing and Louie

knew it would soon be time to wake Algy. Worn out and dreading what the day would bring she stretched herself and shivered in the chilly morning air. Taking Janet's hand she held it tightly as if trying to press some of her life into the still little body. To her relief Janet opened her eyes, murmurerd "Mummy", then fell asleep again. Wondering if she would dare to ring the doctor so early she tiptoed from the room. The good doctor made Mill Farm his first port of call that morning and after examining Janet turned to Louie. "This is not the diptheria," he said. "She is paralysed down one side, it must have been caused by the injection."

"Is that good news or bad," Louie asked, but he was non-committal. "I will come back this afternoon," he said after administering Doreen's daily injection, her bottom resembling a pin cushion, but she was still very ill.

Dr. Pullen had retired and though this young man was very efficient Louie wished it was their old doctor, but when he returned in the afternoon he assured her that Janet was on the road to recovery, the feeling was coming back, and Edwin and little Wilfred would not have diptheria so badly as they had been treated so promptly. Then she had more faith in him.

As soon as the children had recovered, the Council sent men round to fumigate the house and give the family the all clear to mix with people again.

There was no question of Edwin going back to school, he was nearly fifteen. His father allotted him a milking stool and he was soon helping at most jobs on the farm except the horses. There was no way he could get near a horse without starting to wheeze, the cows having the reverse effect and often he would take his breakfast into the cowshed for relief. He worked from morning until night, hoping that his father would pay him even a little wage, but none was forthcoming.

"You shall have something when I sell Highfield. You have a good home, be thankful for that."

Doreen loved dairy work, apart from riding the pony Algy had bought for the two little boys, which had proved too big and strong for them. So Janet and Doreen delighted in riding Tommy any spare moment they had, and Doreen was happy when she was in the dairy churning the butter and patting it into shape. She would have loved to milk a cow but her father would not hear of it. "I am not having her in the cowshed picking up swear words from the men," he told Louie.

"But she can pick them up from you, and there can't be many others."

He would not be persuaded, so when Edwin read an advertisement in the local paper, for someone required to manage a herd of Guernsey cows, two pounds a week and a farmhouse, Louie suggested he try for it. "There is plenty of furniture here you could have and Doreen could keep house and do the dairy work." To his astonishment he was accepted.

It was a charming Cotswold stone farmhouse in the village of Brighthampton and they moved in full of enthusiasm and tried not to be dismayed when Ron, the only other employee, who attended the horses, had a bet with Edwin that they would not last a fortnight, their employer being a notoriously difficult man to work for. Undaunted they set to work to smarten the place up.

Each morning the boss's daughter came to collect the churns of milk in a van and they made sure everything was shipshape and Bristol fashion when she arrived.

The job that Doreen hated the most was washing the cows' udders ready for the milking machine, sometimes having to break the ice on the water trough and apologising to the cows for the cold wash, her own fingers frozen to the marrow.

Most of the cows were sweet tempered and Doreen adored them. When they came in from the field, they all knew their own stall. True their names were on the wall but if they very occasionally made a mistake Edwin would tell them off. "Can't you read?" he would say as the cow shamefacedly shot out and into her own stall. There was one cow that Doreen never really trusted, she had had a calf and was in a loose box on the other side of the yard. Edwin told Doreen to go and milk her, she obeyed, no way would she let him know she was scared, but she left the door ajar in case she had to make a quick exit.

"You really should not let Doreen milk Daisy," Ron told Edwin one day. "She be a funny 'un, I wouldn't really trust 'er."

"She seems alright," Edwin replied but he did not mention this conversation to his sister.

One morning, Doreen was having difficulty lighting the boiler and it fell on Edwin to milk Daisy. Hearing shouting coming from the yard she ran out in time to see Edwin making a hasty exit from the loose box, with the milk pail following him being bunted by the angry Daisy. Ron stood by the stable door with an 'I told you' look on his face.

Once she had checked that her brother was unhurt apart from his pride, she went back to her chores and to her relief she was never asked to milk Daisy again and she noticed that the loose box door was left slightly open when Daisy was being milked.

After a fortnight, Edwin won his bet from Ron and they settled happily into their new lifestyle. Edwin took Doreen into Witney to the pictures, riding pillion on his motorbike was a great thrill to her and to go to the cinema for the first time in their lives gave them both immense pleasure, they resolved to go as regularly as funds would allow.

One of the disadvantages, as well as the paraffin lamps to be filled every day, was the bucket 'lav' across the back yard, Edwin hated the task of emptying it. He always waited until after dark when he would take a lantern and a spade and go into the field at the back of the house. One night when he was executing his most hated task he was so busy digging the hole, he did not hear footsteps approaching. When someone spoke so close behind him he nearly fell into the hole. "I wondered what was going on". It was the village policeman, he had spotted the lantern out in the field whilst doing his rounds and decided to investigate, to Edwin's embarrassment.

"Someone has to do it but it is not my favourite pastime," he

147

grinned. "Will you come back to the farm for a drink and meet my sister?" This offer was gladly accepted, and a glass or two of their Mother's home made wine cheered him on his lonely vigil.

Doreen joined a girls' club which was held in the Stanlake village hall. She really looked forward to the weekly meetings, they did keep fit exercises and dancing, learning the latest steps and enjoying the company.

At Christmas time they organised a party, inviting the boys' club who in turn invited them to theirs. She made so many friends, a very special one was a young farmer's son who worked on his father's farm. He was about Edwin's age and very popular with everyone.

When he asked Doreen for a dance at the party she was shy at first, she had only danced with girls at the club. "I am not very good," she stammered.

"Neither am I," he said, as he took her hand and walked her on to the floor. She soon realised this was not true and could not believe it when he danced with her most of the evening and at the end of the last waltz asked if he could walk her home.

Edwin never joined the boys' club, he was so dedicated to looking after his cows that he rarely left the farm. One of his daily tasks was to walk the bull round the yard for some exercise. A wooden pole with a hook on the end which was hooked to the ring on the animal's nose was advisable when leading a bull but after some time old Billy seemed so docile that Edwin felt he would be more comfortable with just a halter. After a few days, Ron spotted the halter and strongly advised Edwin to use the pole. "He is much happier in the halter." Edwin stroked Billy.

"Happier than you will be if he turns on you. Don't say I haven't warned you. You wouldn't be the first he 'ave put out of this yard". Edwin stubbornly continued to use the halter until one sunny afternoon, Doreen was weeding the front garden when she heard a strange snorting noise coming from the adjoining yard. She stood up and looked over the wall, and there was Edwin running faster than she had ever seen him, with his beloved Billy in hot pursuit, such hot pursuit that his horns were perilously close to Edwin's backside. Her first instinct was to laugh but soon realised that her brother was in serious danger. Grabbing her gardening fork she ran to the yard gate and held it out to him hoping Edwin could catch it as he ran by. Sadly he missed and did another circle of the yard, the next time to her relief he managed to grab the fork. Swinging round to face the angry bull, holding the prongs of the fork toward him, thankfully Billy stopped in his tracks and Edwin stood his ground and lightly touched him with the fork to let him know who was boss. This angered the bull, but he turned away and kicked up his heels snorting and bucking. Edwin sprinted for the gate and had just made it to the other side when the bull turned to make another charge.

Edwin spotted Ron coming from the stable, he knew to his cost that he should have heeded his warning and could not expect any sympathy from him, but Ron was not a vindictive fellow and as Edwin lay gasping for breath was soon by his side asking if he was hurt. Edwin gave a wry grin, "only my pride thanks to Doreen's gardening fork, but it is time I listened to you Ron. How are we going to get the old devil back in his pen?" he asked.

"How are *you* going to, you mean." Ron winked at Doreen and pretended to walk away. "He will go in when he be hungry, then we will nip and shut the gate if we be quick."

"Well Edwin is pretty nippy today, I am sure he will manage that," Doreen teased her brother. "I have never seen him run so fast, well I have never seen anyone run so fast if it comes to that."

"I am going to suggest a nice cup of tea. I will put the kettle on while you get your breath back." Like it or not Billy was never exercised without the pole again. Edwin had learnt his lesson.

They had been at Brighthampton over a year when Edwin announced at breakfast that he was going into Witney that morning. "I am going to see the boss. It is time he gave you a small wage, he can't expect you to work for nothing for ever. Well there is no harm in asking," he added.

Doreen hoped he would be successful, her breeches were

getting threadbare and she would love another dress to alternate with her one and only best dress. "How did you get on?" She ran out to meet Edwin on his return.

"He said he will think about it, but knowing his reputation I don't hold out much hope."

The next morning when the van arrived to collect the milk, Edwin was handed an envelope. As soon as he had loaded the milk and the van was on its way, he opened it with Doreen waiting in anticipation. "The bugger, it's the sack," he said. He rarely swore, but they had worked so hard and all for this, just a week's notice. Doreen fought back the tears. She had been so happy at Brighthampton.

"Ron was right" she said. "He's always right, but I shall miss him," Edwin replied. "I think I will go and tell him just to hear him say 'I told you so'."

"The dinner is ready so don't be long." Doreen went back to the kitchen with a heavy heart, she knew how sad Edwin would be, he had lived for his herd of cows and like herself had become very fond of them. When he came in, Edwin said Ron had heard that a farmer at the nearby village of Southleigh was looking for a herdsman.

"I will go there this evening, it is not far."

He was promptly taken on. The farmer said he knew of his employer and if he had been over a year at Brighthampton that was good enough recommendation for him. There was a cottage with the job but unfortunately no work for Doreen.

When they arrived at Southleigh and saw the cottage, Doreen's heart sank, it was a semi-detached farm worker's cottage with a well and privvy at the bottom of the garden and only two strands of wire to divide the overgrown narrow strips of garden. She tried desperately not to let Edwin see her disappointment, busying herself about the house, but that night she cried herself to sleep.

The next day when Edwin returned from the farm after milking time and sat down to his breakfast, Doreen could see he was not very happy. "How did it go?" she asked. "Not very well. I am not used to being bossed about and I don't know about you but I hate this cottage."

When a few days later Doreen looked out of the wlndow to see her Mother's car stopping outside she tried not very successfully to look happy. "Do you like it here?" Louie asked.

"Not very much," Doreen admitted near to tears, "and Edwin doesn't either."

"I am so glad because I have come to ask you to come home. Your father is very poorly and he must rest, we need help."

"I am sure it will be alright with Edwin, he may have to work the week out though." She felt as if a weight was lifted from her shoulders and longed to be home with her family.

"We will come as soon as we can," she said as she poured the tea. "I think I am a snob Mum, I hate being watched by the neighbours every time I need a bucket of water, and that well gives me the shudders."

Louie laughed, "Well it won't be for much longer, and it will be good to have you home."

Edwin came in for tea looking tired. "Where did you get the flowers," he said sitting up to the table.

"They are from Mill Farm. Mother has been and she wants us to go home. Daddy is not well and they need us." She looked anxiously at Edwin. "Do say you will go."

Edwin was silent then, "Do I have any say in the matter?"

"No."

"Of course I will go, as soon as I possibly can." He stood up. "Let's go into Witney, Dor, there is an Eddie Cantor film on at the Palace and we could have fish and chips afterwards."

"Can we afford it?"

"Just about if we go in the shilling seats. We may not be able to go for a while when we get home." He knew his father would not be forthcoming with his wages but like Doreen he looked forward to being with his family.

They had been home a month and Algy's health had improved when Doreen went into the scullery one evening to find Edwin polishing his shoes. "Are you going out?" she said, rather surprised. He was usually too tired when he had finished work.

"Yes," he said, "how do I look?"

Doreen studied him. "Very smart, it must be something important."

"It is, but promise not to tell anyone."

"Cross my heart and hope to die."

"Well I am going to Filkins to see Mr. Stafford Cripps. I have found out that he owns that piece of land with the gravel pit opposite our gate and I am going to try to rent it from him."

"You are brave, I would not dare."

"Well, I have an appointment, he can only say no, so there is nothing to lose."

"What will you do with it?" Doreen looked puzzled.

"I will tell you when I get back. Can't stop now."

His Mother had always instilled in him never to be late for an appointment. "Where will I say you have gone if Mummy asks?"

"Just say you don't know." He mounted his motor bike and accelerated off at great speed. When he arrived at the house he felt a little nervous as he pulled the big iron bell and heard it ringing in a distant part of the house.

He stood wondering if he should have gone to the back entrance when the door was opened by a maid. "I am Edwin Hutt, I have come to see Mr. Cripps."

"Yes, he is expecting you, please follow me." He was shown into the library. Edwin looked round, his eyes lighting up with appreciation, he loved books, his asthma caused him to spend many days in bed so from a very young age he was a real 'book worm' and was gazing so intently at the rows of beautifully bound volumes that he had not noticed his host enter the room.

"I see you are interested in my books."

"Yes sir, you have a wonderful collection." They sat and talked for a while then Edwin spoke in all seriousness.

"I expect you are wondering why I have come, Sir?"

A moment's hesitation. "Yes, I suppose I am curious, unless

152

you are thinking of joining the Labour Party, but you are rather young," he added thoughtfully.

"I am afraid I am not very interested in politics," Edwin answered, wondering what his father would say, and remembering with amusement hearing him refer to Stafford Cripps as that Labour bloke from Filkins. "My parents vote Conservative but that is not why I am here. I wondered if you would rent me your field with the gravel pit on the Bampton road opposite our farm gate."

There was a stunned silence. "I am wondering what a schoolboy would be wanting with a small field, especially as his Father has a sizeable farm". "I have left school sir," Edwin replied "and I work for my Father, but I would like to start a pig farm of my own."

He talked eagerly about the breed of pig he hoped to keep etc. After much deliberation, Mr. Cripps said, "Well I have no use for the land, so I don't see why you should not use it." He really did not see how he could refuse this ambitious lad.

"What about the rent, sir." Edwin looked expectantly, suddenly dreading the answer in case it would be more than he could afford.

"We will talk about that in a while, when you are on your feet, if you promise to come by and let me know how you are getting on, but rest assured it will only be a peppercorn rent."

Edwin thanked him profusely and was about to take his leave when Mr. Cripps added. "Edwin, if you would care to borrow any books from this library you would be very welcome.

"I would love to, Sir, but I don't think I will have much time for reading, unless you have one about pig keeping," he added with a mischievous grin.

"I am afraid that is not a subject I have been interested in."

It was dark when Edwin mounted his motor bike. As he made for home, he wondered what his Father would say. He felt sure his Mother would be pleased for him but he did not expect any help or encouragement from his Father. But he resolved he would not give him cause to complain about his work.

The girls were in the kitchen preparing the supper when he reached home. They looked at him expectantly. "I've got it," he burst out, hardly believing his luck.

"What are you going to do with it," said Doreen as she rescued a pan of bubble and squeak from the range which had started to burn. I am going to start a pig farm," said Edwin with all the confidence in the world.

"But you haven't any money have you?" She thought for a minute. "There are our money boxes. I have three pounds in mine, you can have it."

"And mine, Janet joined in."

At that moment Louie came into the kitchen. Edwin was soon telling her about his plans and what had transpired that evening. "I have let your Father have most of my money but we will think of something".

She felt proud of Edwin having the initiative to even contemplate starting his own business at the age of sixteen and resolved to give him all the help and encouragement she could.

"When are you going to tell your Father?"

"Now," Edwin stood up. "I'll get it over with." He knew his Father would not be over pleased as he expected him to be working all day long and would know he would have to take a little time to look after his own pigs. "Don't be long, will you, supper is ready."

Louie wondered how Algy would respond but did not have long to wait. Edwin soon came back. "He only grunted," he said, in answer to his Mother's enquiring look. "I don't think he was very pleased." Algy came into the kitchen and took his place at the head of the table. He hardly spoke during the meal.

After supper Louie followed him back into the sitting room. She took the poker and pushed the smouldering logs together encouraging them into a cheerful blaze. "I take it Edwin has told you his plans?"

"If you mean about him keeping pigs, yes."

"Well, what did you think," Louie persisted.

"Its a crazy idea. Who is going to look after them when he is in bed with an asthma attack?"

"We will cross that bridge when we come to it, but first how are you going to help him?" Algy fell silent. "He has worked hard for you with no pay, the least you can do is to give him a couple of pigs to get him started." Algy opened his mouth to protest, but Louie was already heading for the door. "I will call him in and you can tell him."

"Yes Muver?"

"Your Father has something to tell you."

Algy closed the *Farmer and Stockbreeder* magazine he had been reading. "Your Mother has talked me into giving you a couple of pigs to start you off." With that he opened his magazine and continued to read.

Edwin open mouthed with astonishment thanked him and turned his gaze towards Louie, who was concentrating on darning a sock. "I expect Edwin has told you he is going to specialise in breeding Large Whites, so two of those in-pig gilts would be nice."

Algy's face was getting redder and Edwin feared his Mother had gone too far in asking for his prime stock and was about to beat a hasty retreat back to the kitchen when he heard his Father say, "Alright, I will pick you a couple out when you are ready for them." Edwin could not believe his good fortune.

A week later the postman delivered a parcel to Mill Farm directed to Edwin Hutt, Esq., there were curious glances from the family as he slowly removed the wrapping paper to reveal a book on pig keeping. There was a short note hoping he would find it useful and signed Stafford Cripps. He passed it to his Father who, on seeing who had signed the note, glanced at it and passed it back with a barely audible 'very nice', but his Mother was so pleased for him and proud that such an eminent personage should go to so much trouble for her son.

Farming times were hard and many farmers were being made bankrupt, some found other means of boosting their finances. Algy had the idea of letting the trout stream and as most people wanted to stay the weekend Louie decided to turn the farmhouse into a guest house and accommodate the fishing gents and their families. Algy loaded milk churns into the back of his car and with the family piled on the back seat he and Louie set out for Nailsworth, a town in Gloucestershire on the Cotswolds where there was a trout hatchery.

They had never seen so many fish, minute to enormous, in separate pools. The young trout were caught in nets and counted into the milk churns and Algy, delighted with his purchase, drove home with unusual care. They all watched eagerly as he carefully released the silvery little fishes into the brook and saw them darting for the cover of the reeds.

The first guests to come for the fishing came from Warwick, father and mother and two sons about Edwin's age who were more interested in the farm animals than the fishing and spent much of their time playing with the pigs on Edwin's now thriving little pig farm and helping the girls feeding the pet lambs.

Doreen and Janet loved cooking and enjoyed helping their Mother in the kitchen, they shyly and rather awkwardly waited at table but these charming guests soon put them at their ease and after a couple of weekends they asked if they could eat with the family, so extra leaves were put into the large dining table and Donald and Wilfred promised to be on their best behaviour. Mr. Hardwick was secretary at Windsor Castle and they often brought a cake or fancy sweetmeat made by the cook of that celebrated establishment. All in all the letting of the fishing was a great success. Louie and the girls found themselves looking forward to the weekends.

The two women got on well and Algy to Louie's relief behaved himself and enjoyed showing off his fishing skills and helping Mr. Hardwick, and the children really looked forward to the boys' company.

The vicar's wife was having a party for her eldest daughter's birthday, though the vicar was Church of England, Louie suspected his wife may have followed the Catholic faith as they seemed to have a baby every year. The big rambling vicarage echoed with the sound of children's voices.

"Don't need to have a party," Herby said to Doreen one day, "they have a party every day at the vicarage with their own brood. She asked me if I knew anyone who would make a birthday cake and I said I would ask you. I know you be a good little cake maker. She would pay, of course."

"I don't think I would be good enough." Doreen was hesitant, although the idea appealed to her, she loved icing cakes.

"Of course you would miss, I will tell her you will do it."

Donald and Wilfred were invited to the vicarage party and Doreen and Janet were roped in to help. Louie drove them in her little Austin 10 car with the cake in the boot. Doreen was feeling very nervous in case the vicar's wife did not like it but she need not have worried, the good lady was highly delighted and insisted on giving her ten shillings. A few days later the 'phone went and someone else wanted a birthday cake and gradually as word got around and orders came in Doreen found herself enjoying her new hobby which afforded her with a little pocket money.

Janet had now left school and as she was interested in needlework it was decided that she could be apprenticed to a ladies' outfitters in Witney and could travel daily on the train and as Donald and Wilfred were now old enough to start school she could look after them on the journey.

The boys settled happily into their new school but as the weeks passed it was evident that Janet was not happy and at last admitted defeat, sitting on a hard chair all day gave her such pain in her bottom that although enjoying the sewing she could stand it no longer. A prominent Witney family needed help with their two little girls and Janet thought she would like to do that. She would have to live in as family but she rather fancied it especially when she saw the beautiful house.

She was soon missing her sister and brothers in spite of all the splendour, but worst of all she was hungry, she missed the ample farmhouse fare she had always been used to. In desperation she took the two children, one in the pram while the older girl walked by her side towards the town where there was a baker's shop. You could smell the delicious aroma of fresh baked bread before you reached the shop. She bought three penny currant buns giving one each to the little girls, who, like herself, soon tucked in. Now she really looked forward to her afternoon walk until one day, a neighbour spotted the trio coming along the street eating buns. Well brought up young ladies never eat in the street and she lost no time in telling Janet's employer, who severely reprimanded her, especially for giving the children buns and possibly spoiling their tea.

The following week her Mother and Doreen called to see her and Louie sensed at once all was not well. When they were alone Janet tearfully told them, "It's all very posh but there is not enough food."

"I am not having a child of mine going hungry; go and pack your things." Janet did not need a second bidding and with Doreen's help she was soon down with her little case.

"I am taking Janet home, she is not happy." The two girls scrambled into the car after bidding goodbye, Louie started the engine and headed for home.

"Do you think Daddy will be angry," said Janet.

"Not if he knows you were not getting enough to eat," said her Mother, "but you had better keep out of sight until I have told him."

To everyone's relief Algy was in a good mood that evening and was really upset to hear that Janet had been so hungry.

The next morning Louie called the two girls into the kitchen and while she was kneading the dough for making the bread she told them of an idea she had. "Doreen's cakes are selling well," she said, "and you two are both good cake makers. If we put my little car as a down payment for a van and you take your home made cakes round and sell them door to door, what do you think about that?"

There was silence, then Doreen pointed out that when they

158

were out her Mother would not have a car. "But you would be at home baking some days, then I could have the van."

"But we couldn't just knock on people's doors," Janet protested. "Of course you can, they can only say no, and once they have tasted your cakes I bet they will want more."

So it was agreed, and they took the little Austin to a garage who allowed them seventy pounds against a new Austin Seven van costing one hundred and twenty-five pounds, the girls to pay off the difference at twenty-five shillings a week from, hopefully, their profits.

Janet was not old enough to drive but Doreen had passed her test and was thrilled at the prospect of driving their smart little van. A new car had to be run in and it was advisable not to drive over thirty miles an hour. Fearful of what might happen if you ignored this advice Louie and Doreen strictly adhered to the 'running in process' but as soon as the required miles were clocked up Doreen, egged on by Janet, tried it out for speed along the bendy country road from Black Bourton to Bampton, actually achieving sixty miles an hour. The little van was fitted with shelves to put the trays of cakes on and at last they started out with their wares.

Doreen stopped the van outside a row of houses in the next village of Alvescot. They looked at each other.

"Bags you go first, you are the oldest," said Janet. Doreen tapped timidly on the first door. The lady did not answer immediately and she was afraid the door would be shut in her face but it was a bright sunny morning and a deviation from housework was an inviting prospect.

"Would you care to look in the van and see our selection of homemade cakes?" She nodded and followed Doreen down the path and on seeing the array of cakes so attractively displayed soon took advantage of the offer of a 'baker's dozen', thirteen for a shilling.

The girls were delighted and by the end of the morning so few cakes remained they decided to head for home, knowing the remainder would be enjoyed by the family.

A week later Algy burst into the kitchen. "Missus, what do you think," he sat down into a chair, "there are some men out there looking around. They say they are going to make our farm into an aerodrome."

Louie continued to roll the pastry, "You do talk nonsense. If this is an excuse for a cup of tea, you will have to wait until I have finished making this pie."

"If you don't believe me, look out of the window."

There, sure enough standing in the front drive were three men, smartly dressed, carrying brief cases, deep in conversation. Louie stood transfixed. "They can't just take it, can they?"

"I don't know," Algy replied. "They would have to pay, I suppose."

Louie looked thoughtful, "Do you think we should offer them a drink or something?"

"I will ask them, they may tell us if they are still interested." Algy walked purposefully towards the three gents and Louie, watching from the window, saw them shake their heads, so guessed they were not divulging their findings. She went back to her pastry-making, wondering how long it would be before they knew, and if they took their farm for an aerodrome what would they do. Algy came back looking rather crestfallen. "They were not very forthcoming and said they hadn't time for a drink," he said, sinking into a chair and accepting the cup of tea.

The weeks went by with no word from the Ministry. Then one day, Mr. Cradock their neighbour 'phoned Algy to tell him that he had had confirmation that it would be his farm that would be taken for the aerodrome. It would come to the boundary of Mill Farm. "What will you do," Algy asked the old gentleman.

"I don't know, retire I should think," he replied, "but I have not had time to consider. This is all a bit of a shock."

"Well I don't know how I feel about aeroplanes flying over my farm but we will cross that bridge when we come to it. At least I have still got a farm."

Work soon started on what was to be called Brize Norton Aerodrome, though the main entrance was really in Carterton.

To Louie's surprise she had a visit from an airforce officer who had been making enquiries in the district to find accommodation for the captain of the new aerodrome and his batman until his house was built. "I have been given your name. He needs to be near to the 'drome and this would be ideal."

After much deliberation and consultation with the family, Louie agreed and the good captain was finally installed at Mill Farm. His batman was very helpful. Louie and the girls prepared his meals and the young airforce lad waited at table and looked after his every need, advising Louie about the foods he liked and disliked.

It was evident to Louie that Edwin and his father were not getting along. He was now paying rent to Stafford Cripps but to get his meagre wage out of his father was like drawing a hind tooth. "He does not give me time to go to the 'lav'," he complained to Doreen, but he was determined not to be beaten, until one morning he had been up all night with asthma and had dropped off when it was nearly time to get up, thus oversleeping. When he entered the cowshed three pails of frothy fresh milk stood by the door. Before he could speak his father stood up and from the other end of the cowshed shouted, "Where have you been you lazy bugger."

"Please don't swear until I have explained, father." With this Algy picked up his milking stool and with all his force threw it at Edwin who ducked just in time and it clanged against the door. The men's heads were peering from the hindquarters of their respective cows with looks of astonishment and expectation. Edwin picked up a pail of milk walked up the cowshed and threw it over his father, then, placing the pail on the ground, he ran for the door, leaving a very angry father indeed and a stream of unrepeatable swear words.

He burst into the scullery. "Whatever is the matter?" Louie emerged from the kitchen and could see at once something was seriously amiss.

"I have done it now, Mother, I have thrown a bucket of milk over father, I will have to leave home."

He explained to his Mother what had happened. If it was not so serious you would have to laugh, Louie thought. It sounded like a circus act with the clowns doing their slapstick capers, but she knew Edwin was right, it would mean he must leave home. Algy would never forgive him that was for certain and the other certainty was Edwin would never get the wages he owed him and he needed the money to get some more food for his pigs to tide him over until he sold them.

Louie and the girls devised a plan of action, there was plenty of pig food in the granary but when he went out he always locked it and took the key. They told Edwin their plan, he at first protested that it would be stealing but they pointed out that he was owed it, which he had to agree.

"Dad I have just seen old Molhern flying towards the Spinney." Doreen knew he would soon be off anxious to protect his precious trout. He grabbed his gun and some cartridges. As soon as he was out of sight Doreen backed the little van up to the granary and a bag of barley meal was popped into the back. It was quite a walk to the spinney and by the time Algy returned the van was back in its place and the girls were back to their cake making.

The imagined sighting of the heron enabled Edwin to feed his pigs for a few weeks until he could sell them. He put an advertisement in the *Farmers Weekly* for a job and received fifty-two replies. After much deliberation he decided to accept an offer to manage a herd of pedigree highland cattle with showing high on the agenda. When he left home with his worldly goods in a suitcase strapped to the luggage rack on the back of his motorbike, Louie watched as the motorbike disappeared from view and wondered if he would ever return to Mill Farm or see his father again. Algy had known the time Edwin was departing but was notably absent, so Edwin undaunted went in search of him and eventually found him sitting on a bag of meal in the granary.

"I've come to say goodbye, Dad." He approached his father

with outstretched hand, wondering if he would take it. Grudgingly, to Edwin's surprise, he did. They shook hands and then Father and Son stood for a few minutes in silence neither knowing what to say.

Finally, Edwin just said, "Goodbye, Dad," turned and walked away.

When he joined the family in the drive Louie looked at him enquiringly. Edwin nodded. "I've said goodbye." *He does not resemble his father,* Louie thought. None of the children had inherited Algy's red hair, little Wilfred's hair was so blonde it was almost white, while Donald's was dark brown and the three older children were what Louie called 'mousey' brown. As she stood and looked at Edwin saying his goodbyes to his brothers and sisters, she thought how handsome he had grown, his blue grey eyes usually full of laughter now looked sad.

"Take care of yourself and be sure to use the pole if you exercise the bull," whispered Doreen as she hugged him.

When the motorbike was out of sight Louie suggested that they go to Minster Lovell and get some plums. "Herby says they are selling them for a halfpenny a pound if you pick them yourself."

After the first world war the government built lots of bungalows on about two acres of land each to enable ex-servicemen to make a living. Many planted fruit trees now mature and resulting in a good season to a glut. "If we make lots of jam you could sell it on your cake rounds."

Donald and Wilfred scrambled into the van with the baskets. "Watch out for the wasps," Doreen warned them as they set about gathering the luscious fruit.

"Can we go down to the ruins when we have finished," said Donald. A visit to Minster Lovell usually ended up down by the ruins of the Manor House beside the River Windrush, the children loved it there as did the grown ups. It was a mystical place with its legends and in such a delightful setting.

"I am afraid we must go," said Doreen at last. The goats will need milking and Mother will be wanting some help with the cooking."

The girls had acquired two nanny goats and a billy, Milkwell Merryface, Marigold and Max. Marigold had produced twin kids. They were quite adorable, which is more than could be said for Billy, his body odour had to be smelt to be believed. They bathed him to no avail. His long white fur, though he looked cuddly, fairly exuded the disgusting smell.

Algy forbade them to keep him anywhere near the house, so they tethered him on a long chain near the brook and kept a special old coat to put on just to move the tether each day and bring him in to his cosy bed in the goat house.

When the kids were fully grown the girls advertised them for sale and a gentleman came all the way from Andover to buy them He told Louie and the girls that it was a scheme to help ex-servicemen. They were given an acre of land and a goat in some parts of the country. "I will pay fifteen shillings for any nanny goat," he said. "Just put it on the train and we pay the fare."

The girls were quick to take him up on his word and any spare time they had they rode off on their bikes looking for goats. They decided they could see into people's gardens better from a bicycle. They were tempted to keep their purchases themselves but they knew the difficulties they had in keeping Merryface and Marigold away from the fruit trees, they would chew the bark if they had half a chance thus killing the tree and understandably angering their father, so it meant that they put a collar and lead on their purchases and walked them the three or four miles to Alvescot station, often with little gangs of children bringing up the rear, begging, "Please can we stroke him, Miss." Not wishing to go into details regarding the sex of the goat they allowed them a quick stroke.

"A good thing it isn't a him," said Janet. "Their parents might not have appreciated the way they smelt, its lucky the nannies do not smell."

The aerodrome was taking shape. The married quarters and the captain's house were nearing completion. *We shall miss the captain,* Louie thought, but knew he would soon be taking up residence in his lovely new house. Some developers were building a row of shops with flats over in the middle of Carterton and Louie heard through the captain's batman that a cafe was urgently needed as soon as the station opened as there would be nowhere for the lads to get a snack in the evenings. "What about it girls," said Louie, "Shall I buy one and you girls could run it?"

The next day after much deliberation and viewing the shops, Louie decided to buy the first two adjoining shops so that the girls could continue their cake making in the second kitchen.

Algy was getting ever more bad tempered, sometimes sulking and not speaking for days. One day when Louie had taken the two boys and Janet into Witney to do some shopping, Doreen had stayed at home to cook her Father's dinner, which he ate with relish saying little until he had cleared the last scrap of apple pie from his dish. "Where has your Mother gone," he suddenly asked Doreen.

"Into Witney to get the boys some shoes. Didn't she say?" He grunted and rose from the table. She knew her Mother would have told him but he would not have listened. "Are you alright Dad," Doreen ventured.

"No, I am not alright. I have had enough. I am going down the fields to blow my brains out." With that he took his gun from the rack and strode out of the house leaving Doreen aghast and feeling very frightened and alone.

She went into the yard to see if any of the men were around and found Walter in the cowshed. Tearfully she told him of her father's threats. He stood for a minute in silent thought, then said, "Don't eh worry, Miss Doreen, it takes a lot of courage to do that and I don't think the master has quite enough."

"I only hope you are right," Doreen replied but as she spoke there was the sound of a gun shot coming from the direction that Algy had taken. She looked at Walter too frightened to move.

He put his hand on her shoulder. "He has most likely shot a rabbit," he said, "don't you worry."

"Had we better go and see?" she asked hesitatingly, hoping he would say no.

"Just you go indoors, Miss Doreen, he will be back." She cleared the dinner table in a daze and was washing up the plates when the back door opened and her father walked in holding a dead rabbit in his hand, just as Walter had predicted. She hurriedly turned her head and carried on washing up.

He shall not see I have been crying, she thought. He did not speak but walked through to hang the rabbit in the outhouse, giving Doreen the opportunity to swill her face, then she slipped out of the back door to tell Walter he had returned. He just smiled, "I knew he would but he had no call to frighten you like that."

"Do you think I should tell Mummy?" She waited while he considered.

"No, I don't think I would worry her if I were you."

"Alright." She turned to go back into the house.

"Oh, Miss Doreen, you will find a letter in the milk can."

Doreen blushed. "Thank you, Walter."

The girls had met two Airforce boys at a dance and had dated them a couple of times. They had told their Mother but did not dare to tell their father knowing he would forbid them seeing the boys. They could not always get out of camp for one reason or another, so they arranged to send a message with Walter.

She ran to the back door and took the letter from the milk can. It was addressed to her and on the back of the envelope were the letters S.W.A.L.K. She hadn't a clue what it meant but after reading the short note arranging to meet that evening, she took Walter out a mug of tea.

He looked at her with a knowing grin. "Sealed with a loving kiss, eh?" Doreen laughed.

"The silly ass," she said, angry with herself for not knowing what it meant, while even Walter knew, but was glad she had found out when they met the lads in the evening.

"Shall we walk to Clanfield and have a drink at The Plough?" said Arthur tucking Janet's arm through his. Doreen and Paddy followed, he put his arm round her and they strode along in the gathering dusk.

Paddy broke the silence. "I meant it, you know."

"You meant what?"

"What I put on the envelope."

"You hardly know me, and don't do it again, my Mother might find out."

"You knew what it meant then?" Doreen nodded. She and Janet had had a good laugh about it and decided he was a soppy thing, but ever after the same initials were on the back of Paddy's letters in spite of her protestations.

Louie was kneading the dough, a task which she enjoyed, seeing the dough rise and the eventual smell of the cooked loaves of bread as she took them from the oven.

The telephone was ringing and as she wiped her floury hands and ran to answer it, her look of expectancy turned to anxiety. The girls ran to her side when they heard her ask the caller which hospital is he in, guessing it must be Edwin. "I will come straight away," she said as she replaced the receiver.

"Edwin has been attacked and gored by a bull," she told the girls. "It was in a field, it ripped his shirt off and he had to be rescued by two men with pitchforks, they say he is lucky to be alive."

"I will see if your father will take me to see him," she said, running from the house, only to come back looking crestfallen. "He says he is too busy, one of you will have to stay and look after the boys and everything."

Doreen knew it would be her and though she longed to see Edwin resigned herself to carry on making the bread and cooking the dinner while Janet accompanied her Mother.

"I will 'phone you as soon as I know anything" Louie said, kissing Doreen goodbye.

They found him in a sorry state, though typically making light of his injuries. "He is lucky to be alive," the Matron reiterated "but he is a very plucky young man. I am told he saved himself by holding the animal's horns until he was rescued." Edwin had lost consciousness and the Matron beckoned Louie and Janet to follow her. "You will want to telephone home," she said, ushering them into her office. "You can tell them we are confident that he will soon make a full recovery. If you would like to stay tonight, there is a small hotel quite near to the hospital we recommend." Louie thanked her and said they would like to do that.

The shock and the long drive to Lambourn was beginning to have its effect and Louie sank gratefully into the proffered chair as a young nurse entered the room with a tray of tea and the news that Edwin had regained consciousness.

"Mother has 'phoned," Doreen told her Father at dinner time and hesitated, hoping he would ask how Edwin was, but all he said was "Oh yes," and started eating his meal.

"They are going to stay the night as he is very ill." He did not answer.

"Will Edwin come home when he is better?" asked Donald. Algy was silent so Doreen just said, "I don't know Donald, but it would be nice," but she knew in her heart he would not be coming.

Edwin lodged with the farm manager and his wife and was very happy with them, that evening they came to see him. They had not been married very long and it was evident that they looked on Edwin as not just a lodger but a real friend. He was feeling a little better by the time they arrived but short visits only were allowed, giving Louie and Janet a little time to get acquainted with Mary and Ron, who promised to keep them informed of Edwin's progress if they went home on the morrow, as they intended to come into the hospital every evening. Louie and Janet finally made their way to the hotel and bed.

Though very comfortable, Louie found it impossible to sleep, the events of the day turning over and over in her mind and longing for the morning to find out how Edwin was feeling. So now hurt and bitterness with Algy for not coming with her to see Edwin magnified as she lay there in the darkness.

Doreen was serving the dinner when they heard the crunch of car wheels on the gravel drive. Wilfred jumped from his chair and Donald followed and were about to run out to welcome their

Mother and sister when their Father in a loud angry voice told them in no uncertain terms to, "sit still and eat your dinner".

Doreen did not dare go out but knew how sad her Mother and sister would be at not being met after their journey. When, after what seemed an eternity, Louie, followed by Janet, came into the dining room, all the children, ignoring their Father's orders, ran to her with cries of "How is Edwin?" but Algy went on eating his dinner and did not speak a word. Louie hesitated before answering to see if her husband would show any concern but none came. *How could he be so heartless,* Louie thought. *I don't think I am going to be able to continue to live with him,* and as the days passed and Algy's temper and sulking did not improve, she made up her mind that something must be done.

Mr. Farant, Louie's solicitor, listened patiently as, near to tears, she poured out her troubles. After much thought and discussion, it was decided a legal separation must be the answer.

He explained to her that it would mean going to court and the children would have to go to say which parent they would rather live with, which would be quite an ordeal for them. The little lads were fond of their Father and he them. They were at the right age to enjoy shooting and fishing and all the pursuits that young boys living in such a delightful environment were privileged to pursue.

EIGHT

On her homeward journey, Louie began to have doubts about them choosing to live with her. That evening Algie was in such a bad mood that Louie made up her mind and told him she would be leaving him. This did not improve matters and sent him into such a rage she thought for a moment he would resort to violence but he stamped out of the house slamming the door behind him. She now decided to tell the children. "We shall be taking possession of the shops next week," she told them, "and I shall be coming with you girls as I am leaving your Father."

It was make up your mind time as the children trooped into the Abingdon Courthouse but without hesitation they all chose to live with their Mother and they were soon to move to Carterton.

The modern flat was such a contrast from the rambling farmhouse but they were so busy getting the cafe ready that there was no time for regrets. Donald and Wilfred were to attend Burford Grammar School as boarders. All were relieved to be living free of Algy's increasing violent tempers. Louie searched her conscience long and hard before taking the final drastic step and did not leave him until she had found a suitable housekeeper, she felt sure he would not behave towards a stranger as he did with his family.

The girls were excited about opening the cafe and they all hoped against hope that there would be enough trade but their fears were unfounded. The word quickly spread at the camp and the 'boys in blue' or as some people dubbed them 'the Brylcreem boys' were soon wending their way towards the cafe. The aerodrome was designated to train young pilots, conseqently there was the occasional accident. Louie and the girls were usually the first outside the camp to hear who had 'pranged' and what damage had been sustained both to pilot and plane.

They are so young for such responsibility, Louie thought. She knew in her heart that Edwin would eventually be in uniform but remembered his prediction when he was a small boy that it would be the navy for him though at present he was very happy breeding and showing cattle having now completely recovered from his accident.

There was to be a Ball in one of the huge hangers at the camp causing great excitement for miles around. The girls, with the help of a friend, made themselves a new evening dress for the occasion. When the day came and Paddy and Arthur arrived at the cafe to escort the girls to the dance it was to find the cafe so packed with customers that many were waiting for tables. "I don't know how we will be able to come," said Janet disconsolately, "you will have to go without us." But as she spoke, the boys, as one, took off their coats and headed for the sink to tackle the ever increasing piles of washing up.

Louie emerged from the cafe with a pile of dirty plates in one hand and the goldfish bowl in the other. "What is the matter with Tommy," asked Doreen relieving her of her load.

"Flying Officer Meredith was absent-mindedly stirring the fish with his fork. I think he has had a drink or two. Poor old Tommy was swimming round ninety to the dozen, don't let Wilfred know." Wilfred had won him, or possibly her — one would not know with a fish — on a visit to Bampton Fair in a rifle shooting competition. He, like his Father, was an excellent shot.

It was nearly nine o'clock and the girls had resigned themselves that there would be no dancing for them that night, when a cheery face appeared at the back door in the form of Mrs. Gatz, a good friend and neighbour. she had heard through the grapevine how busy they were and decided to offer a helping hand. "Go get your glad rags on girls," said Louie, "we will manage now."

As she spoke, a car horn sounded. "That will be Duck's

Disease," said Arthur.

"What do you mean, Duck's Disease," asked Louie.

"That is his nickname, he doesn't mind." Duck's Disease was the proud possesor of a new Morris 8 car and spent most of his free time polishing it.

As they neared the hanger the strains of *Alice Blue Gown* were distinctly audible, and when they entered, the sound of the band and the shuffling of hundreds of feet on the concrete floor echoing in the vast building and the colourful spectacle of the ball gowns was something to behold. They stood for a while marvelling, then Duck's Disease said, "I will be back shortly to claim a dance," and strode off towards the stage. As they watched, the band struck up, Duck's Disease took the proffered microphone and in a clear strong voice crooned the next number to the tumultuous applause of the dancers.

"I didn't know he could sing," said Paddy. "

And how!" said Arthur. "I have only heard him in the ablutions but not taken much notice."

After another curtain call, Duck's Disease came towards them smiling. "You're a dark horse" said Janet.

"Yes, and may I have the next dance?" and before she could answer she was being led on to the floor. "The cheeky little devil," said Arthur, "but he did give us a lift, so I won't complain."

To Doreen's surprise she saw the handsome figure of Captain Robinson walking towards them and more surprised were Paddy and Arthur when he said "Hello Doreen". They had no idea she knew their Commanding Officer. When he asked her for a dance she felt very honoured, though worried if her dancing would fall short, but as the band struck up she soon found herself falling in to step and chatting happily with the Captain. He told her he missed being at the farm in spite of having a lovely house with all mod. cons., enquired about the family and said he would come and visit the cafe soon. Doreen did not mention that her parents had separated. "Didn't know you knew the Captain," said Paddy when they were alone.

"There is a lot you don't know about me, but you are learning. Right at this moment I just hope Duck's Disease will give us a lift home. I am feeling very tired."

As she spoke, he came towards them and suggested they get away before 'God Save the King' to avoid the crush. Doreen looked crestfallen. "I like the Anthem," she said, "it would be a finale to a perfect evening."

"You will have to walk home then," said Duck's Disease "unless you have the last dance with me."

"That's blackmail," said Paddy, but did not exactly relish the walk so relented with a good grace. They all agreed it had been a wonderful evening as they piled into the Morris 8 and headed for home.

A year had passed. There was so much to do that the days flew by. Then one evening a man came into the cafe and it was evident that he had been drinking heavily. He was tall and broad and Janet felt at a glance that he looked menacing as he stumbled in the door. She was cleaning the tables, but quietly slipped out to the kitchen where Doreen was cooking. Louie had gone to see their good friend Mrs Gatz promising not to be long.

"I think we have trouble," she whispered, pointing in the direction of the cafe.

"I will serve him." Doreen picked up a tray. Telling Janet to "wait here" she walked hesitantly through the door and approached the man now sitting at a table. He looked up enquiringly through bleary eyes.

"May I take your order," Doreen said. There was silence. Doreen waited patiently, then he said in a slurred voice, "For starters, I will have a kiss."

"This is a cafe not a restaurant. I am afraid we do not do starters."

Silence again. Then, "How many will I get for a main course?"

"I am afraid they are off today. Shall I ask the chef to do you a nice ham and eggs?" She thought if she mentioned the chef he would think there was a man around. "Shall I get you a cup of coffee while you make up your mind," and before he could answer she walked with as much speed as she could without running, into the kitchen. Janet had been listening at the door. "What shall we do?" she said.

"He is big, isn't he? Too big for us to cope with if he gets obstreperous. Tell Donald or Wilf to go the back way and fetch PC Tandy and pray no one comes into the cafe." As she spoke she poured a cup of coffee from the percolator and took it in to the man.

The police house was almost opposite, the boys sensing the urgency in Janet's voice ran quickly only to be told by his wife that the constable was out on his rounds. "Go to the Laurels and fetch Mother and ask if Mr. Gatz could come and help," said Janet when they returned. "Tell them to be sure to come in the back door," she added as they ran off.

The girls stood wondering what to do next when there was an almighty crash coming from the cafe. The man had banged his fist on the table sending the coffee crashing to the floor. "Oh our lovely china," Janet gasped.

"That's it!" Doreen went to the cupboard and took out a clothes line. "He may be on the large side but there are two of us and we are sober, you ask him what he wants to eat and keep his attention." She put the rope on a tray and a cloth on top of it, pretending to wipe the tables. She went behind him, and while Janet spoke to the man she quickly put the rope round his ample body, pulled it tight pinning his arms to his sides before he realised what was happening. The girls then pulled his chair from under him landing him on the floor. Round and round went the clothes line rendering him quite helpless. Janet opened the door and they dragged him out of the cafe, leaving him on the pavement, then ran in bolting the door behind them.

As they stood wondering what to do next, the back door opened and PC Tandy came in. "The wife said you wanted me," he said "so I came straight over."

"Yes, you had better come and see." The girls led him through the cafe and pointed to the bundle on the pavement in the gathering dusk.

"What in the devil?" The constable walked towards the prostrate man. "What has been going on?" He turned to Doreen. "I am afraid we cannot have that behaviour in our cafe, Mr. Tandy. You were not at home so we dealt with him ourselves, he is very drunk indeed."

"Look at our china," Janet chipped in pointing to the broken china and pools of coffee.

The constable looked thoughtful, "But how?" he pointed to the man. "You didn't?"

"We did," Janet answered proudly. "What will you do with him" asked Louie who had followed the constable in, accompanied by Mr. Gatz and the two boys.

"I'm blowed if I know." He tilted his helmet back and scratched his head thoughtfully. Then a subdued voice came from the bundle. "I promise if you untie me I will go quietly. I'm in agony here and I want to . . . ."

"Alright," Mr.Tandy quickly intervened.

He looked at Louie. "Go on," she said, "I don't think he will bother us again." They watched him as he walked unsteadily off without a backward glance.

Later that evening, to the children's dismay, Louie told them that she had made her mind up to sell the cafe and take them down to Weston super Mare and buy a guest house. "This evening has confirmed my fears, this business needs a man about."

"But we managed him," Doreen protested. But despite all the begging and cajoling, Louie's mind was made up and she would not be dissuaded and the very next week she put the cafe on the market.

The girls were devastated, the thought of leaving all their friends, especially Arthur and Paddy, and go so far away appalled them but they knew their Mother was determined so finally resigned themselves.

Donald and Wilfred were sorry to leave Burford School but to live at the seaside held a certain allure. The girls decided to tell their boy friends the next evening, so after Louie and the boys had gone to bed Janet burst out. "We have got something to tell you."

"We have got something to tell *you*," Arthur said, looking very serious, "but ladies first."

So Janet told them of their impending move. When she had finished, Paddy said, "Well our move is very similar. We are to be posted. Arthur is going to Rhodesia to train to be a pilot and I am being sent to Stranraer on a course."

"But why Rhodesia?" Janet looked puzzled. "I thought they trained pilots here."

"Yes, but I am going to fly bombers."

"Why, we are not at war?"

Arthur and Paddy exchanged glances. "There are ugly rumours of happenings on the Continent, but don't let's think about it."

Arthur gave Janet a little hug. "We will never see each other again," said Doreen.

"Of course we will," Paddy reassured her, and we will be sure to write often. Promise you will."

"I promise," but she knew in all probability they would never meet again.

The next few weeks were a whirl of activity, the cafe was sold, and Louie bought a house at Weston-Super-Mare. It was a large solid stone house in a residential part of the town. They soon had it ship shape ready for guests, the boys were fixed up with a school close at hand and the girls were settling in to their new surroundings but missing the hubbub of life at Carterton.

"I think I will put an advertisement in the Lady," said Louie "and one or two in the local papers." But the weeks went by and no replies. She soon realised she had made a mistake to buy a house so far from the town and sea front, but did not mention her fears to the children.

"The milkman told me there is a hotel on the Locking Road

where they sell butter and they have several vans delivering it. I will go and see if they have a vacancy for a driver, there is no sense in us all waiting for guests." Doreen looked at her Mother for a sign of approval.

Louie nodded. "Good idea, we will not get any guests until the Spring." It was early December, a wet and windy morning, but undeterred Doreen boarded a bus and headed for Hill View Farm Hotel. The door was opened by the proprietress, Miss Spencer, who asked Doreen to step in out of the rain before enquiring the nature of her visit.

She came straight to the point. "I was told you sometimes have vacancies for van drivers and I need a job."

Miss Spencer looked thoughtful as she eyed Doreen up and down. "I am afraid we do not need drivers at present."

"I hope you didn't mind me asking."

Disappointed, she turned to go, but before she had reached the door Miss Spencer said, "I am clutching at straws here, but I suppose there is no possibility that you can ice cakes? I have made thirty Christmas cakes and have no time to ice them."

Doreen told her about their little cake enterprise, adding "I am only very amateur," but she was quickly ushered into Miss Spencer's sitting room. After a short while she was taken to the dairy and introduced to Mr. Mansfield, Miss Spencer's partner, who was in the process of making clotted cream, while four girls, dressed in white were mixing butter in what looked like cement mixers and patting it into half pound pats. Mr. Mansfield was a middle aged man with a pleasant almost jovial expression and Doreen took to him at once. On the way back to the house she said, "I noticed Mr. Mansfield is very lame, did he have an accident?"

"Yes, he did," Miss Spencer told her, "he was up a ladder and a lorry accidentally backed into him. He is lucky to be alive."

Everything was settled, she was to have sixteen shillings a week and all her food and start the next morning. "You will take your meals with Mr. Mansfield, myself and Molly, she is our receptionist, you will like her. Come and meet her." She was five or six years older than Doreen with a figure so dainty and a step so light Doreen felt she should have been a ballet dancer or some such. Her hair was straight in a swept back style which enhanced her twinkling blue eyes and welcoming smile. Doreen already felt at home at Hill View Farm but supposed it would only be until she had iced the Christmas cakes.

Louie was pleased for Doreen and had news of her own to tell her when she arrived home. "I have had a reply to the advertisement," she said. "A gentleman needs a home for his Mother who is semi invalid, he is going to bring her next week."

Janet was scanning the newspaper. "I will get a job too," she said. "Someone needs an assistant in a cake shop in the Boulevard. I will go in the morning to try for it."

Dreading that her efforts at icing the cakes would not be up to expectation, Doreen was relieved when Miss Spencer seemed pleased with her day's work, even more relieved when the vans returned next day and reported that all the Christmas cakes were sold.

Janet started work at Miss Wraysons cake shop in the Boulevard, and the following week Louie's paying guest arrived, bag and baggage. She seemed quite a sweet old lady and her son seemed pleased to get her settled in, promising to visit often, but the next day Louie's worst fears were realised. It was quite evident that she would need more nursing care than she was qualified to give. "She is sitting up in bed picking the blankets to pieces," she told the girls that evening. "She will have to go or I will have no bed clothes left". Janet took her supper tray up that evening and sure enough she was so busy methodically dismantling the blanket that she did not hear Janet enter the room. "I don't think I am having much success with my paying guests" Louie said as she picked up the 'phone.

Doreen had finished icing the cakes but found herself roped in to help run the busy hotel kitchen, to her relief nothing was said about her leaving. Then about a week before Christmas, Miss

Spencer said, "Doreen, Mr. Mansfield and I have been wondering if you could cook the Christmas dinner this year. There would be fifty guests in the dining room and the staff. Mr. Mansfield would roast the turkeys and help with the carving and I will see to the drinks, planning the courses, and cooking would be your responsibility. Don't answer now, have a night on it."

"You are quiet this evening, Doreen," said Louie.

Doreen told her about Miss Spencer's proposition, "I have to give an answer in the morning, and I am not sure that I can do it. Fifty people is a lot."

"Of course you can do it." Louie went to the bookcase and selected two or three cookery books and without more ado they were planning different dishes. Miss Spencer breathed a sigh of relief when, next morning, Doreen agreed to her proposal and set about making Christmas puddings. She was liberally pouring brandy into the mixture when Phylis, the kitchen maid sidled up to her. "May I have a stir, Dor, I really need a bit of luck." Doreen handed her the large wooden spoon and wondered if the bulge under her white apron would have the decency to not put in an appearance until after Christmas.

Phylis had joined the staff at Hill View Farm on leaving school and had proved a good worker. Unfortunately a date with the young coalman and a walk in Kewstoke Woods only once, was once too often. Miss Spencer tried to persuade her to tell him but she would have none of it and when there was a coal delivery to the hotel she hid in her bedroom and would not come out until he had gone. So arrangements were made for the baby to be fostered and Phylis to visit it on her days off.

The Christmas dinner proved to be a great success and by now Doreen had taken over the main cooking for the hotel leaving Miss Spencer more time to make cakes to be sold on the vans.

"I have had the vicar round again," Louie said one evening. "He keeps trying to talk me into going back to your Father. He says I am wicked to have left him, reminding me of my marriage vows. I have told him I will think about it."

179

A few days later there was a letter from Edwin. Louie spotted the postmark and her heart sank. "Portsmouth. You open it," she said, passing it to Doreen who opened it and handed it back to her Mother.

"Its really for You." She, like Louie, had guessed its content. *Dear Mother,* Louie read, *as you have seen by the address I have joined the Navy. I expect you realise our Country is on the brink of war and even though I was in a reserved occupation, I intend to fight for my Country. I have been turned down twice because of my asthma, but third time lucky.*

When Louie had finished reading the letter, Janet, who had been very quiet asked, "Do you think there will be a war?"

Louie shrugged her shoulders. "We can only hope and pray that it won't happen."

"Edwin always had such faith in the League of Nations," said Doreen. He joined when he was in his early teens and always wore the badge on his lapel.

The following week Mr. Mansfield asked Molly and Doreen to join him in the sitting room. Doreen had never seen him in such a serious mood, his usually happy smiling face was pale and drawn. "There are dreadful things going on on the Continent," he started, "things that few people in this country know about. Hitler is persecuting the Jewish people, there are plans afoot to smuggle some out of Germany and I am one of many hotel owners in Weston to volunteer to employ one or two. They come from wealthy families and will not be used to menial work, so I want you to be as helpful as you can. They will probably have lost their families and be very unhappy."

"Do you think there will be a war, Mr. Mansfield?" Doreen asked.

"I am afraid so. We cannot let Hitler carry on as he is."

Edwin is right, she thought. a cold shiver went down her spine as she thought of her brother going to sea and how vulnerable ships must be. Though she had little concept of what happened in war apart from the knowledge that it was no longer bows and arrows used as weapons, she, like many other people, had no idea of how ill prepared her country was. So when Mr. Chamberlain stepped from the 'plane after visiting Germany, waving that famous piece of paper declaring there would be no war, everyone breathed a sigh of relief and went on with their lives.

The two German girls arrived at Hill View Farm with little ceremony. They were both about twenty-three or four and very attractive. They were not related and were not acquainted, having only met on the journey to England. Their names were Elsa and Lisa, they had very little luggage, but Doreen noted that the clothes they wore were without doubt, very expensive. They looked sad and bewildered. Doreen's heart went out to them and she wondered what was going on in Germany to cause such unhappiness. But little was known and the girls themselves had no knowledge of what had happened to their families, only that they had been taken away.

"The vicar has been round again," Louie told the girls one evening. "He has talked me into going back to your Father. I have had a letter begging me to return."

After much discussion the girls decided to get a bedsitting room and stay at Weston, they were both happy in their work and had made lots of friends. The boys would have to go back to the farm but did not seem too unhappy at the prospect, so when the house was sold the girls found a bedsitting room for twelve shillings and sixpence a week in the Locking Road, which was about half way between the Boulevard and Hill View Farm.

"Well, it is not Buckingham Palace," said Janet as she surveyed the big iron bedstead, but there was a French window which led to a small back garden and the landlady seemed a pleasant soul.

Soon after they had moved in and Louie had gone back to Algy there was a letter from Edwin to say he had some leave and would rather not go to the farm, not being sure of what sort of reception he would get from his Father. He would like to bring a mate who lived in Scotland and was not keen to make the journey. Mrs. Meade agreed to let them have a room. Her husband was a retired Petty Officer so she had a soft spot for Navy lads and made them very welcome. Edwin and his friend had finalised their training and had a short leave before going to sea, so everyone did their best to make it a happy time.

HMS Berwick was Edwin's first ship and he wrote that he was enjoying the life. It was a great surprise when a few months later war was declared.

Doreen's first realisation of how serious was the situation, was when she saw a crocodile of very young children walking down Locking Road from the station two by two, holding hands, each with a little box hanging round their shoulders containing a gas mask. They had been evacuated from London and anyone who had a spare room was compelled to take one in. Some were lucky in their new homes and found kind and loving foster parents. Some, of course, were not so fortunate, but their safety was the first priority as the bombs began to fall mainly on the big cities.

Louie wrote to the girls to try to persuade them to get a job nearer home and sent a newspaper cutting with an advertisement for two girls to bottle milk at a dairy in Oxford with a flat supplied. They decided to apply and wrote off that very evening.

When a letter came two days later to say the job was theirs if they could start in a fortnight, they looked at each other in astonishment. "I don't know how we can leave at such short notice," said Doreen. "I will hate to leave Hill View Farm in any case."

"I don't know what Miss Wrayson will say, but I think we ought to go," Janet replied. Miss Spencer and Mr Mansfield both did their best to persuade Doreen to stay, offering to double her wages, but understood their dilemma. She finally said her tearful goodbyes as did Janet and Miss Wrayson. "I only hope we are doing the right thing," said Janet, as they boarded the train. Their very dear friend Edith came to the station to see them off. They had struck up a friendship just passing on their way to work, a friendship that was to last a lifetime.

The flat was over a corner shop selling the dairy produce and in the pouring rain looked from the outside rather drab and uninviting but the door was opened by a middle aged lady with a kindly face who explained she and her son Sidney, aged ten years, would be living with them and would look after the flat but they would do their own cooking. Mrs Simmons was a widow and the girls loved her from the start. She was 'Simmy' to them from day one. "I hope we can manage the work," said Janet. "I think we will like it here."

When they arrived in the yard next morning, dressed in white overalls and wellies, they met Arthur the manager who explained the work to them. At first their hearts sank, the heavy churns of milk had to be manhandled down some narrow wooden planks from the building above the yard, then the milk had to be tipped into a vat above the bottling plant. "We will never manage it," Janet whispered, but Doreen gritted her teeth and took hold of a churn.

"We will have a jolly good try". She pulled it towards the planks but as she looked down, she envisaged the churn tipping over long before it reached the bottom. They half lifted, half slid it to the yard below and looked up to see the manager watching, and Doreen thought she detected a look of surprise. Men had always been employed but had been called into the armed forces.

Simmy came down into the dairy armed with two bowls of soup and dumplings. "How are you getting on," she asked. "His nibs was sure you would not manage, but it looks as if you have proved him wrong. He is not a bad sort. I think you will get on alright with him."

A few weeks had elapsed and the girls were settling into their new home when, one evening, Doreen answered the door bell. There on the doorstep was her Mother and clambering out of a taxicab was Donald and Wilfred. Simmy and Janet had followed her to the door to hear her say that Algy had turned them out of the house in one of his rages. He would not allow her to get a coat or her handbag. Simmy and Janet took them in while Doreen paid the taxi man.

The next morning Louie realised to her concern that Simmy had given up her bed for her, the boys and girls had improvised. "I am going to Abingdon," said Louie at breakfast time. "Our friend, Mr. Blagrove, is a house agent. "I will find a house to rent and take in paying guests."

"Not again," said the girls in unison. But not deterred she boarded a bus to Abingdon to seek the help of Mr. Blagrove who took her to see the only sizeable house to rent on his books, as people were moving out of the cities, some already being bombed out.

Prospect Park was outside Abingdon on the Wooton Road. It was situated up a long drive with Wellingtonia trees in the grounds. In spite of needing a coat of paint, it was quite impressive. It was rather near to Abingdon Aerodrome but as Louie said, "Beggars can't be choosers."

"I will take it," she said. "Don't you think you should have a night on it."

Mr. Blagrove looked serious. "It is a very large house, Mrs. Hutt, quite an undertaking."

"I have made my mind up. I am not going back to Algy. How soon can I move in?"

"Next week, I should think. It has been empty for some time. The owner will be pleased to get a tennant."

After a cup of tea and a chat with Mrs. Blagrove she returned to Oxford with mixed feelings.

Was she right to decide so quickly? "He who hesitates is lost," she quoted to herself, "well there is no going back now."

She arrived back at the flat to find the girls cooking tea for Donald and Wilfred and was soon telling them about Prospect Park. "I know you will like it," she said at last, "but there will be a lot of work before we can take paying guests."

"The rent is two pounds a week, which is reasonable for such a large house. I suppose the reason for that is it being so near to the aerodrome."

Arthur, the manager, called Doreen into the small office one morning and confided to her that in the evenings he worked for a milk bar in George Street. "I wondered if you would like to work there for a few evenings a week, it would be about six shillings for the week." Doreen jumped at the chance. "Could Janet come too," she asked. "Not at the moment, they only need one, perhaps later on."

There were two milk bars in Oxford. They were very popular, especially late at night, for theatre goers to have a nice hot drink before going home. Doreen enjoyed working there, she was the youngest of the staff who, apart from Arthur, were all women. She was particularly fond of Mrs Lee who did the washing up. She was plump and always cheerful and actually appeared to enjoy her work. Her hands were red with constantly being in soda water, washing soda being the only ingredient to soften the water before the invention of detergents and 'hands that do dishes in the sink' were not usually 'as soft a your face' but she never complained.

By the time the last customer had departed and they had cleared up and had a hot drink themselves, the streets of the City were almost deserted except perhaps for air raid wardens and policemen. Even though she was invariably very tired she enjoyed her walk home. The girls found that if they worked hard they could finish the milk bottling by lunch time and decided if they had some means of transport they could get over to Abingdon and help their Mother in the afternoon. It was a toss up whether to get a second hand car or two bikes.

Doreen mentioned to Arthur their intentions. "I will introduce you to Jack West, he deals with cars and comes in most nights for a glass of hot milk and some 'Dads Cookies', always the same."

It was nearly closing time when Arthur called Doreen over and introduced her to the young man on the other side of the bar. "You can serve him then you can tell him what you want." Doreen poured a glass of hot milk and placed it on the bar together with a plate of 'Dads Cookies'.

"I did not tell you what I wanted," he said. "It's a well known fact, one could say a standing order," she said. He smiled and dunked his biscuit in the steaming milk.

"My sister and I are thinking of buying a car but we have not got very much money. Arthur said you may have one, it needn't be posh".

He swallowed the rest of his milk, noticing Arthur waiting to lock the door."Will you be here tomorrow?" She nodded. "Goodnight then, see you tomorrow," and he was gone. The next evening it was close on closing time when Doreen spotted him in the crowd making his way towards her. She passed him his order. "I think I have got a little car that will suit you," he said, handing her the money. As he spoke a lady came towards her to be served and she did not get the chance to speak to him again. She was still serving customers when she saw him leaving. "He might have waited," she said to Arthur who was standing near. "He says he has a car for us."

"He will be in tomorrow," Arthur replied absently.

The staff finally trooped out into the unlit street but this night a full moon shone on a very smart sports car standing by the kerb. "Would you like me to give you a lift home then we can arrange for you to see the car?"

She was so taken aback by surprise she did not answer. But after a moment's hesitation, she stepped in. "This is nice," she said.

"I like it, I have a particular love of Jaguars," he replied. As they drove through the now almost deserted streets towards Walton Street and on to Kingston Road, Doreen tried to question him about the little car he had to show them but he would not be drawn. "You will have to wait and see, I will show it to you tomorrow."

The girls were watching expectantly at the window the next afternoon, when into view came the dinkiest little Austin seven, nineteen twenty-nine vintage, with its hood down, being driven by Jack at some considerable speed. They rushed out to meet him, Arthur had spotted him from the shop and came out to join them. "I like it," said Janet. "We will call it Askeytoff the second". The girls had been to the cinema the afternoon before and had

186

seen a comedy film with Arthur Askey calling his car Askeytoff.

"Steady on, we don't know if we can afford it." Doreen turned to Jack who thought for a moment.

"Do you think you could manage fifty shillings, two of the tyres are a bit smooth, but it has a good engine."

"Do you really mean two pounds, ten shillings?"

"I think it is worth that," he said apologetically.

"I meant, is that all, do you really mean it?" He nodded, "As long as you give me a lift back to Iffley Road."

"And as long as you can give us a cup of tea before you go," said Arthur heading for the flat door.

That evening Doreen and Arthur discussed the little car, "All I can say is he must have got a soft spot for you to sell it for that price," said Arthur.

"I could well have a soft spot for him, but I expect he is married," she said.

"It so happens he is not and he has just come in." Doreen turned round to see him heading in her direction and hating herself for blushing.

As they drove home, Jack asked if she would like to go for a drive on Sunday. "I have a friend who would make up a foursome if Janet would like to come." So it was arranged and on a gloriously sunny afternoon they set off in the direction of Henley in the SS Jaguar. Arnold and Janet were getting on well. Arnold was a fine figure of a man with dark hair and brown sad looking eyes, a gentle manner and softly spoken.

The girls had packed a picnic, so when Jack stopped the car by the river and suggested they hire a boat and have their teas on the river bank the girls were thrilled, assuming he was as adept at rowing as he was at driving.

They all clambered into the small boat. Jack took the oars, but it was soon evident that rowing a boat was not his forte and the little craft, caught in a current, was going round in circles. "I don't think I am any good at this," he conceded at last, by which time they were in the middle of what looked to Doreen like a very wide river. The girls had been rowing boats at Radcut Bridges but that was much higher up the Thames and the river there was much narrower.

They looked at Arnold. "Can you?"

"I have never been in a boat before, leave alone rowed one."

"We know how," said Janet amid fits of laughter. Standing up she moved on to Jack's seat and grabbed an oar.

"You will tip us over in a minute," said Arnold, "and I can't swim."

"You are joking, of course," said Janet, but noting the look on his face realised it must be true. "For Heaven's sake be careful. I don't fancy having to lifesave him," she said, as Doreen changed places with Jack and took the other oar. It was some minutes before they could make any headway but finally they got into a rhythm and headed up the river at a very slow rate.

They passed may beautiful houses with gardens running down to the river, some looking a bit neglected, the war already taking its toll. Although farm workers were excused National Service, gardeners were being conscripted. They finally came to open fields and deciding that would be far enough managed to manoeuvre the boat to the bank.

The picnic was a great success. Simmy had helped them pack it. "The way to a man's heart is through his tummy," she had said. They sat on the river bank talking until it was getting dusk. "You would not think there is a war on, it is so peaceful here," Jack remarked.

"No, but I think there there will be one in Henley if we don't get this boat back," said Doreen.

"I think we have got the hang of this," said Janet as they manoeuvred the boat back to its moorings.

The next day Arthur came into the yard accompanied by a pretty blonde girl a little older than Doreen. "This is Margery," he introduced them, "she will be staying in the flat with you for a few weeks until a flat is ready for her at the stables on the Cowley Road. She is going to look after the horses." These horses were used to pull the pretty little wagons used to deliver the milk. This meant she would have to be away from the flat by three o'clock in the morning to cycle up the Cowley Road and give the horses their breakfast, get them harnessed and ready to go by five o'clock. These carts were now gradually being manned by Land Army girls.

Now that they had a little car, the girls were able to go to Abingdon two or three times a week, and were able to help their Mother in her enormous task of renovating the house and preparing to take in guests.

Askeytoff was a bit temperamental and many times it meant pushing it the rest of the way. It was getting a familiar sight to see two girls pushing the litle car through Oxford late at night, policemen and air raid wardens would have a cheery word.

"I will never be ready," Louie confided on one such visit, "and I don't think guests will want to stay here, the planes come in so close; come and see this". She took them to the back of the house and to their amazement there on the ground was a chimney pot smashed to pieces. "I honestly thought that one had got us," she said. "The boys and I have decided to sleep downstairs for the present."

"No wonder Mother looks tired," said Janet on the way home, as the little car slowly chugged its way up Boar's Hill. "I think it must have damaged the 'plane," said Doreen.

Louie had invited them for lunch on the Sunday. "Bring your boy friends if they would like to come," she had said.

Jack's car turned into the long tree-lined drive. The chestnut trees were in full bloom, alternating one creamy white and one pink on either side. When they reached the house there was Donald and Wilfred in the drive, Wilfred excitedly holding out a black bundle of fluff. On closer inspection they realised it was a labrador puppy. "I knew the boys were missing the farm and thought it would help," Louie told the girls later as they helped prepare the lunch. "Otherwise I think they like it here except for the 'planes of course. They come in so low it is a nightmare for us and must be for the pilots. I worry for them as I do for Edwin on the sea. I don't know which is the lesser of the two evils."

Doreen produced a letter from her pocket. "This came yesterday." It was from Edwin. All letters were censored from the forces so they did not know where he was. He would not have been allowed to say, if he had it would have been blanked out, but there was a snapshot of the deck of the ship so thick with icicles and snow that it was a clear indication of his whereabouts.

"He must be on a Russian convoy," said Janet. "We were so against the Russians before the war and now we are risking the lives of our men to help them."

"But I suppose they are helping us by fighting the Germans, poor things, so there you are," said Louie.

"Will Arnold or Jack be called up?"

"Arnold works at the factory, so he will not, but Jack will soon, but he deals in cars and has scrap cars in a yard in Jackdaw Lane off Iffley Road. Last week he had a letter from the War Office to say they wanted him to put the scrap cars on certain open spaces to stop the Germans from landing so he won't have to go for a while."

Louie took a large pie from the oven. "Your Father allowed the boys to have their airguns, I hope everyone likes rabbit pie."

"It smells good," said Arnold, as the boys trooped into the kitchen followed by the puppy. In the afternoon it was all hands to the wheel clearing a patch of overgrown garden and having a bonfire.

"I will bring my own tools next time, this slasher is Jolly blunt," Jack grumbled.

"There won't be a next time if I don't get a ride in that car," said Louie. He did not need a second asking to down tools and whisk Louie off towards the drive, "I am not much good at gardening," he confessed.

"I could see that, why do you think I suggested a ride?" He laughed and opened the car door with a flourish.

"Your Mother is on the 'phone," Simmy called out to the girls a few days later.

Janet was nearest to the flat. "Can you come over this afternoon?" Louie sounded really worried. "It is imperative that I see you both."

"We will be there as soon as we can." Louie had been watching for the little car and ran out to meet them, "I am so worried" she began as they followed her into the house. "I have had a letter from the War Office to say I must vacate Prospect Park in a fortnight, they need it for a hospital."

"They can't do that," Janet protested. "It seems they can and I have had all the hard work for nothing. I have told Mr. Blagrove and he is going to take me to Oxford tomorrow to try to find a house to rent. There is nothing in Abingdon. I suppose in some ways it is a blessing in disguise. I don't think we could still live here with the 'planes, I have not slept properly for weeks and the boys' schooling will suffer if they don't get a good night's sleep."

The next day, Louie and Mr. Blagrove called at the flat to tell the girls they had found a house, the last and only suitable house to let in Oxford. It was in Bradmore Road on the North side of the City, not far from the University Park which was a delightful place with a duck pond at the far end running down to the River Cherwell.

The next day Arthur told them he had received his calling up papers and would be leaving at the end of the week to join the Army and an older Manager would be taking his place.

The girls had worked out the time it took to do their work in the dairy and found they need not get up too early some mornings, so when the following week Simmy shouted a warning that the new Manager had arrived they hurried out into the yard but were waylaid by a rather stern faced man who they felt at first sight they were not going to like. "Have you just come to work?" he demanded.

"No, we have just been to spend a penny," Doreen fibbed.

"I am the new Manager, my name is Mr. Adams." The girls introduced themselves and he stamped off towards the shop without another word. "I can see we shall get on well with him," said Janet.

"Perhaps he is nervous and trying to assert himself," Doreen suggested.

"He is an old misery guts you mean" Janet laughed. The next few weeks proved her to be right, nobody had a good word for the new Manager.

Louie had settled in to No. 10 Bradmore Road and guests were arriving, many fleeing from the increasing bombing of the Capital, One of the first being Mr Malcolm Campbell with his wife and young son Donald. Oxford had so far escaped the bombs but when Edwin came home on leave he was so concerned to find his Mother had installed a chicken house and pen at the bottom of the garden but no Anderson shelter. "Hitler will never bomb Oxford," she said confidently. "He thinks he will educate his youth here but not if we can help it and I like my guests to have a nice fresh egg for breakfast."

There was a telephone call from the police one afternoon, asking if she could accommodate an ATS officer for a few nights. When she arrived Louie was struck by her beauty, her well tailored uniform so perfectly fitted her slender figure, blonde curls peeped out from her uniform cap and bright blue eyes completed the picture.

"A friend may be calling," she told Louie when she had shown her to her room and about half an hour later a handsome young Army officer was at the front door.

Afternoon tea was served in the lounge and after dinner the young man went up to the girl's bedroom. When she heard the front door being opened and closed at three o'clock in the morning, Louie realised the young man must only just be leaving".

After breakfast she decided to telephone the police. *I don't want them thinking this is a disreputable house,* she thought.

"Someone will be 'phoning you back," said the policeman and sure enough a few minutes later there was a call from the Colonel's office to say he would be calling on Louie. *Well he needn't think I am putting up with shinanigans,* she resolved, and had hardly had time to tidy her hair and take off her pinny when there was a ring at the front door.

There was a camouflaged limousine by the front gate with an Army driver at the wheel. "I need to talk to you in strict confidence Mrs. Hutt," he said, accepting a glass of sherry. "We decided not to tell you but I realise now, we were wrong. Our girl is doing a difficult and dangerous assignment, we have reason to suspect that the officer who visited her last night is a German undercover agent. She has befriended him and is going to great lengths to find out the truth, would you please let her stay for a few more days, she will I am sure, be as discreet as possible."

"Of course," said Louie, "I had no idea."

"Please don't mention it to a soul, remember walls have ears." Louie smiled, those words were on posters everywhere. "I have little time for gossiping," she said.

At the end of the week, the young officer took her leave, Louie was sad to see her go, she had been an exemplary guest and one could say an endearing one, no doubt the reason why she was chosen for this assignment. Louie never knew if she was successful with her mission. In some ways she felt she would rather not know, the young man seemed so nice.

Janet at last received a letter from Arthur. It was a while since she had heard, apparently he had directed her letters to Mill Farm and Algy had not forwarded them. He had finished his training and had returned from Rhodesia and would be going on his first operational flight in a fortnight, to pilot bombers over Germany. He was having a party to celebrate and would dearly love her to come. He lived at Stratford on Avon, his Mother would love to meet her and she could stay as long as she liked.

Janet was upset. "There is no way I can get away," she said. "Old misery guts would never agree."

"Don't tell him then, I can manage for a couple of days. He might not even miss you."

"Are you kidding, he does not miss much."

"Well he could not say anything if the work is done and I will manage."

So it was agreed and Janet left the following weekend. Mr.

Adams was in the shop that morning and noticed Janet was not in the dairy. He casually asked Simmy who was there making purchases where Janet had gone and Simmy had quite innocently let it slip she had gone to Stratford on Avon for the weekend. He did not go into the dairy all weekend and Doreen was thankful that she did not have to tell any white lies. On the Monday when the girls were busy bottling the milk and Janet was enthusing about her wonderful weekend Mr. Adams came striding into the dairy.

"How dare you take time off without asking me," he shouted at Janet, his face red with rage, "you can pick up your cards at the end of the week."

As he turned to go, Doreen spoke up. "You can have mine ready too then, if Janet goes so do I". She saw his face drop and knew that to replace them both at such short notice would not be easy.

"You did not even ask for a explanation," said Janet as he strode off.

"How did he find out," said Doreen when he had gone.

"I am afraid it was me," said Simmy who had come in the door with two basins of soup. "He asked me where Janet had gone, so I thought he knew she had taken time off". Simmy was close to tears as the girls uncharacteristically had not much appetite for their soup.

The girls were looking down the vacant Jobs column in the Oxford Mail. Doreen spotted a vacancy for a man to do a milk round for two pounds a week. Burtons Dairy was near to the Milk Bar so she started off to work early that evening and called in on the way. "I need to speak to the Boss man," she said to the white coated man behind the counter.

"I'm Edgar Miss, what can I do for you."

"I am looking for a job and you are advertising for a man. Are you fixed up yet?"

"No, but it is really a man's job. You would not be strong enough, the electric vehicle is heavy on the steering and you would have to lift churns of milk to deliver to schools as well."

"That is no problem, I am doing that all the time, would you let me try?" It was finally agreed that she be on a week's trial but being a girl he would not pay the two pounds a week and finally agreed to thirty five shillings.

She went to work at the Milk Bar with a lighter heart and when Jack was driving her home, which had become a regular occurrence, she told him the whole story. "We will have to get somewhere to live and horror of horrors I have to get to work at six o'clock which will mean getting up before five."

"I can't think of anything worse," he said, laughing and hugging her.

Margery had moved to her flat on the Cowley Road and told the girls there was a bed sitting room to let just opposite which they lost no time in investigating. It was the most uninviting room you could imagine, but spotlessly clean, so they decided to take it. There were notices everywhere, 'Please refrain from . . .' and 'Don't forget to. . .'

Janet came back from the bathroom the first day. "That is the best one yet," she said. 'Please refrain from standing on the lavatory seat.'

The next day Janet applied for a job at the Co-op to do a milk round and was accepted. "Let's celebrate this afternoon when you get back from work. I will pack a picnic and we could hire a punt and go down the Cherwell. I could see if Margery would like to come." The three girls set off for the boat yard in high spirits.

Margery was fun to be with and always good for a laugh. They were not very expert with the long punt pole but were making headway up the river when they came to a part which was fenced with a high boarded fence. "What is in there," said Janet. There was a small gap at the bottom of the fence and curiosity getting the better of them they leant over the side of the punt and peered under. The sight they beheld nearly caused them to fall out of the punt. A rather portly gentleman was walking towards the water as naked as the day he was born, two more were sitting by the pool and there were several swimmers, some only a few yards from them. They fell back into the punt, Doreen grabbed the pole and pushed it away from the fence and down stream before they exploded with laughter. "That must be 'Parsons Pleasure'. It is a nudist bathing place for men. Simmy told me about it," said Janet "but I did not believe her."

"Why 'Parsons Pleasure'?" asked Margery. "I don't know but it is a good thing sharks don't live in rivers."

"Janet, you are incorrigible," said Doreen pulling the punt pole out of the water. "Shall we have our picnic now. I'm starving".

The girls had now joined the Women's Land Army but were able to stay in their jobs. The uniforms were, unlike the other forces, not very smart but were practical and comfortable. The bib and brace overalls were a joy to wear, the corduroy breeches were extremely comfortable and together with a green 'v' necked pullover and a wide brimmed hat—though as Janet said it was not much of a turn on to go courting in—were, in the days of clothing coupons, a welcome addition to their wardrobe.

Doreen had completed her trial period and was now on her own doing the milk round. She was enjoying the work, the initial stiff shoulders and aching limbs had acclimatised. She had made many friends on the round, and quietly purring along in the electric vehicle in the early hours, listening to the dawn chorus, helped her to forget the terrible war for a short while.

Janet was learning her round with a much older man who had not much patience and she was looking forward to being on her own, but at the end of the second week Doreen noticed she was not her usual chirpy self.

"Are you alright, Jan?"

"No I have got the sack," she replied.

"Why, for goodness sake? You were getting on so well."

"I fell asleep."

"That's nothing, I do it all the time, you wake up when you hit the kerb."

"But I was driving down Headington Hill and that horrid old man reported me."

"Don't worry, we will soon find you another job, that was a funny old place to fall asleep, you must have been going rather fast."

"I suppose I must have been. I expect it did put the wind up him."

"But there was no need to sack you." Doreen hugged her sister.

The next day she was talking to Edgar her boss and mentioned in passing that Janet had been sacked for falling asleep. Edgar thought it a huge joke. "If she could drive a horse and cart my brother would give her a job," he said.

"We were brought up on a farm. I am sure she could," said Doreen.

"Tell her to come and see us Miss." He always called Doreen 'Miss'. *He is a nice man,* she thought.

There was hardly any need for a man to show Janet the round, the horse knew exactly where to stop and where to walk on and she was soon able to go solo with her equine partner. She and Arnold were still "walking out" though having seen Arthur again she found herself thinking more and more about her first love. They had started writing to each other once more and on that unforgettable weekend there was no doubting his feelings for her.

His sister had confided that he intended marrying her but did not dare propose with his uncertain lifestyle. He knew full well that the bomber crews would be very lucky indeed to survive this terrible war. He was doing the thing he had always wanted to, flying, though 'bombs away' time he dreaded, the thought of the destruction and loss of lives was abhorrent to him but the lives of his crew was top priority and he hoped and prayed he would be able to keep them safe.

"When you have finished work tomorrow, can you come round to Jackdaw Lane," Jack said. "I have got something to show you."

Puzzled as to what it could be, Doreen hurried home from work. The girls had purchased two bikes to get to work. She pedalled

197

round to Jackdaw Lane to find Jack under a car, spanner in hand, covered in grease and oil. "It was lucky I have come in my working clothes," she said as he hugged her, then taking her arm, walked down a narrow lane towards the river and there, by the bank was moored a small cabin cruiser prominantly displaying its name 'The Wild Duck' on its side.

"What do you think of it?"

"Why, its surely not yours?"

"I took it in exchange for a car. I thought we could have fun with it this summer, at least until I have to go in the Army."

"Well at least you don't have to row it," she teased.

It proved to be a hot dry summer and lazing on the boat was a joy when they had time. But time for all of them was of the essence, for Doreen and Janet their work was more and more demanding. As the men were called into the forces their rounds were divided into half and given to the girls and before long, what started as one round ended up being two.

They heard of a furnished flat over a tailor's shop almost next door to Margery's. Though it took a large slice of their wages, it was Heaven after their bedsitter. Margery, who was always up first in the morning would come round and wake them and join them for breakfast. She enjoyed cooking and mostly cooked the Sunday dinner while the girls were doing their rounds.

One wonderful old lady, Mrs Gurden, gave Doreen a home made cake every week. She and her husband lived in a lovely old cottage down a lane at the top of Headington Hill and was one of her first customers. On the doorstep under a large upturned bucket was a variety of vegetables from their delightful garden and a cake every Sunday morning. Jack and Arnold usually came to tea at the flat on Sundays, the highlight being 'Gurdies' cake.

On collecting days, Friday and Saturday, they seldom got home before seven o'clock at night and it was on one such evening, feeling tired and hungry it was to find a letter addressed to Janet in a handwriting she did not recognise. It had a Stratford on Avon postmark but was not Arthur's writing. She passed it to Doreen "You open it."

Doreen tried to reassure her but fearing the worst opened the envelope and their worst fears were realised. It was from Arthur's Mother to say he had been killed. She said he was returning from a bombing mission when one engine failed on his way back to base. He had to pass over Stratford and after ordering his crew to bale out, knowing the area, tried to land the crippled 'plane in a field he knew was away from habitation but unfortunately was killed in the attempt.

Paddy and Doreen had ceased to write to each other. Doreen felt it was two-timing Jack to write to an old flame and gradually Paddy's letters stopped coming too.

Louie came to tea one Sunday and Doreen felt there was something she wanted to tell them. Jack had taken her for a ride in the Wild Duck in the afternoon and after tea while they were washing up in the tiny kitchen she told the girls what had happened. "I am ashamed at being so gullible" she said. A gentleman had been staying at the guest house for a month. He was a middle aged man extremely pleasant, well spoken and well dressed. He told Louie he was a director of a big firm in Birmingham and she had no reason to doubt him. He asked if he could pay monthly for his accommodation and she readily consented. On the morning he was leaving, he came to the kitchen where Louie was preparing the breakfast and asked if she could lend him £20 as he was expecting a parcel from the postman which was to be cash on delivery. "I will pay you together with my bill when I have been to the bank." Louie unhesitatingly took twenty pounds from her handbag and passed it to the man who went apparently to meet the postman. Louie was too busy serving breakfast to her guests to notice if he really did. Later in the morning he called through to the kitchen that he was off to the bank. When he had not returned after three hours, Louie mentioned to her daily help that he should not take this long to go to the bank.

"Well his case is in the bedroom, so he will have to come back," she replied.

"Come with me, I don't like this." They ran upstairs to the

bedroom and clicked open the large suitcase. There inside were four bricks and a shabby old book. They looked at each other in astonishment. "I have been well and truly duped," Louie said, as she went to the 'phone to tell the police. "I feel such a fool."

Louie was showing the two detectives the case. "If it is any consolation you are not the only one to be taken for a ride by this Johnny. We will get him eventually but he is a cool customer."

The next day there was a letter from Edwin, his ship HMS Berwick had been bombed and badly damaged. He was to be transferred to HMS Cairo but was coming home on leave for a week first. He wondered if the girls had room for him to stay at the flat. The girls were delighted, they had not seen their brother for some time. Jack and Arnold took them out for a drink most evenings and he spent some time with Jack when the girls were at work helping him and though he jokingly said it was a bit of a come down he enjoyed leisurely trips in the Wild Duck.

One evening after they had gone home and Janet had gone to bed, Edwin and Doreen sat talking until well into the night. He told her of his experiences when the bomb hit the Berwick. He had volunteered as a stretcher bearer which was not a task he had anticipated as the casualties were either mates or at least known to him.

The next night there was an air raid warning. "That wailing thing fairly turns your stomach," said Edwin. "I think I had better go to Mother. I suppose she still hasn't got an air raid shelter."

"No, and you can't go out in an air raid," said Doreen. "She has got Donald and Wilfred, they are very sensible lads, they will probably all get under the stairs."

"Here they come," said Edwin. The night sky was filled with the formidable dark forms of aircraft. "They are German, the engines have a different sound to ours," he said as wave after wave were droning overhead. They had been in bed but were scrambling into their clothes. "I can't find my knickers" said Doreen.

Janet gave a hollow laugh. "Just hurry up, we must get

downstairs." Still no bombs had been dropped. They sat in the little kitchen after making sure the blackout curtains were drawn tightly together and drank endless cups of tea. The next day they heard that Coventry was practically flattened and felt so sorry for the inhabitants of that unfortunate City and hoping against hope that it would not be their turn next.

The months went by and apart from the odd bomb in surrounding districts Oxford was unscathed. The girls were visiting their Mother when the telegram came to say Edwin had been seriously injured and was in hospital in Gibraltar. It transpired that HMS Cairo was in the Malta Convoy when she was torpeoed and Edwin now a leading stoker was one of the few stokers to be saved. He was picked out of the sea with multiple injuries. The wonderful Matron of the hospital wrote a letter every week to tell Louie how he was getting on, and a telegram came from the War Office briefly letting her know how he was progressing.

After some weeks, to everyone's delight, a letter from Edwin to say he was a little better. He had been on the danger list for three and a half months when his latest letter said he was hoping to come home soon.

Doreen finished work early and decided to visit her Mother. She was just in time to join her for a cup of coffee. "You are looking tired Mother, did you not sleep well?"

"No dear, I am afraid I did not sleep at all. A strange thing happened to me last night. I was just going to put the light out and get into bed when standing by the door was Edwin. He said, 'Muver,' and smiled. I went towards him and said, 'Oh Edwin we did not expect you yet. When I was close enough to touch him he vanished into thin air."

"You were dreaming, I expect," said Doreen. "No, I had not got into bed, it was no dream." They had only just finished their coffee when there was a ring at the door. The young lad handed Doreen a telegram. "It is the usual one from the War Office I expect," she said opening the little yellow envelope. Her face blanched.

"I know what it is," said Louie. "Does it say what time he went." Doreen nodded. It was exactly the time that Louie had seen him.

"He came to say goodbye," said Louie, tears streaming down her face.

A letter came from their landlady to say she was coming back to Oxford and would be needing the flat. They had been so happy there and knew it would be almost impossible to find another as more people were being bombed out of their homes in other cities.

Janet, having seen an advertisement for a girl to help a racehorse trainer near Winchester, decided to give it a try. When Doreen told her Mother about the turn of events she suggested that she could live at Bradmore Road for a while. She was feeling so very low after Edwin's death and would love to have her. Though she had a much longer ride to get to work Doreen was able to help her Mother with the guest house in the afternoons and evenings; she had given up her job at the milk bar. She loved helping plan and cook the evening meal, though with rationing it was sometimes a puzzle to know what to cook.

Donald and Wilfred were bonny boys with healthy appetites. Donald was nearly fourteen and had made his mind up to be an electrician. Wilfred, now twelve, was a placid, happy go lucky lad, always full of nonsense and fun.

They cycled out to Abingdon one day and were surprised and shocked to see Prospect Park had disappeared, the lovely old house was raised to the ground. "I suppose it had to go for the safety of the aircraft," said Donald, "but it seems a shame. I wonder what happened to all the vegetables we planted."

"I have sold a car to a very nice lady and she has invited me to have tea with her family on Sunday. She says it is open house and I am to bring anyone I like. Shall we go?" Jack asked Doreen. She agreed. "That will be nice."

"Her name is Mrs. Clarke and I am sure you will like her." When they drove in through the wrought iron gates and up the gravel drive to an attractive modern house and saw a Rolls Royce car and two MGs parked in the front, Doreen felt a little apprehensive. "This is all rather up market," she said. "I would have worn my best dress if I had known."

"You look fine to me," Jack reassured her. Mr. Clarke was a successful businessman and they had two very pretty daughters. One was married and the younger one was a little older than Doreen. She was very sophisticated and beautifully dressed.

Doreen wondered how they could dress so well with clothes rationing, but supposed if you have plenty of money there is always the black market. Mrs. Clarke was a superb cook and in spite of the distinct feeling that their hostess was pushing her daughter towards Jack, even sitting her beside him at the tea table, Doreen enjoyed the afternoon.

The next Sunday Jack said, "Mrs Clarke has invited us to tea again."

"Do you really want to," Doreen asked. "Yes, might as well," he replied.

"Do you mind if I don't come. I promised Mother I would help her in the garden."

"Bye then, see you later," he kissed her and was gone.

To Doreen's surprise, Jack did not come back that evening and as the days went by his visits were less frequent. At first she put it down to the fact that he was busy at work, but as time went by she began to wonder if he had tired of her or found someone new. She tried to tell herself that she did not care but she knew if this was the case she would be heartbroken. Doreen was clearing out her Mother's chicken house one Sunday morning when Jack arrived, much earlier than usual. In fact some Sundays lately he had not even come. "I was hoping to take you out for the day," he said. "Well I won't be long changing," she said, sprinkling some fresh straw on the floor of the chicken house. She was quite convinced he was going to tell her he wanted to end their relationship. Putting off the evil moment, she took her time getting ready.

They hardly spoke a word as the car sped along the Fair Mile towards Henley. Doreen broke the silence, "Are you alright for petrol, this is rather a long way?"

"Yes, Mr. Clarke gave me some coupons the other day." These words set alarm bells ringing in Doreen's head. She thought back to the day they had had tea at the Clarke's house and to Helen their attractive daughter.

Neither spoke until Jack stopped the car at a spot near a wood where the bluebells were in full bloom, the sunlight shining through the trees making dappled patterns on the carpet of blue. They sat in silence for a few minutes, then Doreen said, "I know what you are going to say. It has to do with the Clarke family hasn't it?"

"Yes, it has."

"And you are in love with Helen?"

"No, I am not, nor she with me. I have been going over there a lot lately but it was not to see Helen, it was to repair Mr. Clarke's Rolls Royce. Apparently Helen is seeing a married man who they disaprove of. Mr. Clarke said he would set me up with a garage after the war if I were to marry her. I told him I was engaged to you and hoped to marry you soon." They sat in silence.

Doreen was thinking about Edwin and almost the last words he spoke to her. "I like Jack, Doreen, I do hope you will marry him, I want to be Godfather to your first child." *I know he would be pleased,* she thought.

A squirrel ran up a nearby tree and a cock pheasant strolled through the wood picking his way through the undergrowth close to the car.

"How soon?" she whispered, not wishing to startle them. "As soon as you like. It won't be too soon for me," he answered. "Who knows what the future may hold?"

THE END